Why Are You Here?

A Primer for State Legislators and Citizens

Franklin L. Kury

University Press of America,® Inc.
Lanham • Boulder • New York • Toronto • Plymouth, UK

Copyright © 2014 by University Press of America,® Inc.
4501 Forbes Boulevard, Suite 200, Lanham, Maryland 20706
UPA Aquisitions Department (301) 459-3366

Unit A, Whitacre Mews, 26-34 Stannery Street,
London SE11 4AB, United Kingdom

Library of Congress Control Number: 2014947121
ISBN: 978-0-7618-6462-2 (paperback : alk. paper)—ISBN: 978-0-7618-6463-9 (electronic)

Cover photo: Debate on the death penalty in the Colorado State Senate, Denver, March 11, 2013. In the foreground is Senator Lucia Guzman. Source: AP/Brennan Linsley/CORBIS.

∞™ The paper used in this publication meets the minimum requirements of American National Standard for Information Sciences Permanence of Paper for Printed Library Materials, ANSI/NISO Z39.48-1992.

This book is dedicated to the 7,382 members of
America's state legislatures and their 314,000,000 constituents,
the source of legislative power.

Contents

Introduction:
A Handbook for Action

Figure I.1. Map of State Capitals courtesy of the University of Alabama Maps website. Source: University of Alabama, Dept. of Geography Maps, alabama-maps.ea.edu.

This is more than a trivia question. What do the following headlines from April 2014 have in common?

- Oklahoma botches execution of convicted killer.
- Federal judge invalidates Wisconsin's voter ID law.

- In California, Governor pushes a Rainy Day Fund.
- Florida advances tuition bill for children brought illegally to U.S.
- Gay rights push shifts its focus South and Southwest.
- Georgia approves "unprecedented" gun rights law.

The answer is that each of these headlines is about an emotionally charged subject confronting a state legislature. Each story received national attention. Together they underscore the emerging realization that America's state legislatures have never had more challenging work or been more important to the life of our nation.

America's fifty state legislatures—7,328 elected members supported by 35,000 staff—have a full agenda of state problems to resolve. They also have the challenge and opportunity to fill, at least in part, the legislative vacuum created by the inability of the U.S. Congress to function as our national legislature. (Ironically, the state legislatures also have the power to break the gridlock in Congress by reapportioning their Congressional seats to make them more competitive.)

In doing this work state legislatures have their own problems to surmount. Although not as severe as that of the U.S. Congress, state legislatures are held in low esteem by the public that elects them. The most recent comprehensive poll shows only five legislatures with a public approval rating of better than 50 percent.[1] The state with the highest public approval rating is North Dakota, with 66 percent, and the lowest is Rhode Island, with an approval rating of only five percent. According to a *POLITICO* review in 2010 of publicly available polling data, numerous state legislatures are showing off-the-chart disapproval ratings accompanied by stunning levels of voter cynicism.[2] Even more telling of the public distrust of legislatures is that since the late 19th century, 24 of the 50 states have taken great chunks of legislative power out of the hands of legislators and—at least theoretically—placed it in their own hands through an initiative and referendum process.[3] And fifteen states have placed limits on how long a person may serve in the legislature,[4] a clear manifestation of public distrust.

Yet state legislatures ought to be held in much higher esteem. After all, they are the segment of our federal constitutional structure responsible for governing matters that have great impact on everyday life—such as providing education for our children, protecting our natural environment, assuring public order through the state police and National Guard, building and maintaining highways and mass transit systems, providing care for the needy and deciding such questions as what constitutes a marriage. In 2010 the fifty legislatures approved state budgets totaling $1.53 trillion for these and other purposes as well as $2.7 billion for their own operations.[5]

Just as important, the magnitude and complexity of the issues facing the state legislatures are greater than ever. And the amount of the unfunded pension liability ($3 trillion) and health care liability ($1 trillion) is three times the total of funds appropriated to run all 50 state governments in 2011.

The state legislatures also have great authority over the election process that determines who wields political power, as well as fundamental questions of life and death. All elections, even those for national office such as President and Congress, are conducted by states under state election laws. In the 2000 Presidential election that was eventually decided by the U.S. Supreme Court, it was the Florida state election system that was the focus. Important issues concerning the beginning and end of human life are also within the purview of state legislative power—abortions and the death penalty come to mind.

Legislatures, which have evolved through seven centuries of English and American history, should be viewed as a great treasure of our civilization, but I suspect very few Americans see them in that light. From New York to California legislators are asked to resolve controversial issues under relentless pressure from professional lobbyists and interest groups. Clouds of scandal and misuse of office occur too often and make their work heavier. At home, skeptical, irritated and often angry constituents confront them. Caught between these forces and handicapped by low public regard, the ability of legislators to carry out their responsibilities is fully challenged.

The voting public does not appear to have a sustained interest in the legislatures and how they function, let alone how they should function. A comparable question can be asked of legislators themselves. Do they fully understand the institution in which they serve and their role in it?

The purpose of this book is to provide a practical understanding for legislators and their constituents in the 50 states of the fundamental principles that determine how well legislatures succeed. The book is a primer addressed to both elected representatives and their constituents because the two are inextricably linked. Legislators are the agents of those who send them. The power comes from the constituents and is only temporarily given to their legislators. Legislators who forget this fundamental point can quickly perish at the polls.

Legislatures may be underperforming, but they are also underappreciated. They often function better than the public perceives but not nearly as well as they could. Restoring legislatures to their proper level of public esteem will require persistent effort by the elected members, but it will also need a more consistent, sustained effort on the part of the public to understand and support the legislative process.

When a winning baseball team goes into a losing streak, the manager often tries to restart the team by emphasizing the fundamentals of the game that were neglected in the passions of game. This primer is written in that spirit—to review the fundamentals that are often overlooked in the pressures of the legislative "game" but which are essential if the institution is to succeed.

This book does not seek to be a political science treatise or academic text of the type written by such eminent legislative experts as Alan Rosenthal, Peverill Squire and Karl Kurtz. It is not a book for academic study but a handbook for action. It is designed so that anyone in any state can evaluate their state legislature.

It is not practical to analyze each state in one book and is impossible to make generalizations that apply to all the states with equal validity. This book will not pass judgment on any of the state legislatures or legislators— that will be left to the readers. Rather, the author will discuss several questions common to all legislatures and provide the online websites for each state that provides the necessary information on each state. Readers are asked to use the text in each chapter to focus on the issues and then use the websites and other information sources to see how their state compares to others. With that the reader can do a critical review of his or her legislature and decide what, if anything, should be done to improve it. Rather than use tables and charts printed in the text, the book refers the reader to websites. This is practical because the websites are usually updated regularly and thus stay current.

Since legislatures exist only by constitutional authorization, the first chapter will discuss the development of constitutional government and the significance of constitutions to each legislator and their historical legacy. Chapter One will be followed by a description of the work and nature of legislatures and the role of their members as agents of their district. This chapter will consider the necessity of compromise in the legislative process.

The book will then discuss four issues that are basic reasons for current public distrust of legislatures. Is your legislature seen as more interested in benefits for its members than for the public interest? How does your legislature deal with lobbyists and campaign finance? How does it deal with scandals and ethical questions? How does it handle redrawing of district lines after each census?

These fundamental issues are discussed in a way to engender thought and discussion on often overlooked fundamentals of the legislative system. Provocative questions will be raised, such as, in an era of electronics and instant communication, do we really need legislatures? Is signing a "no tax pledge" compatible with taking an oath to uphold the constitution? Is it possible to govern without compromise?

The closing chapter asks the questions in the book's title to both the legislators and their constituents. Why are you, the legislator, here in the capitol? Why are you, the constituent, here in the capitol?

What should constituents expect from their legislators and, conversely, what should the legislators expect from those who elect them? The last chapter tells of two different efforts to change Pennsylvania government— the Occupy Harrisburg movement and the redistricting efforts of Amanda

Holt, a schoolteacher from Allentown who had a huge impact on the redistricting process. The book concludes by showing how Holt had a significant impact on the legislative redistricting process in Pennsylvania, which provides fundamental lessons for legislators and constituents alike in every state.

Following the text is a "Legislative Tool Box" that contains a list of informational sources, a bibliography and suggestions for additional reading, and excerpts from historical documents important to legislatures.

The book is directed to everyone—Democrat, Republican and independents, liberal and conservative. I hope that readers will find it informative and inspirational. The tasks for legislatures and those who elect them are truly daunting. If the book contributes to success in doing those tasks I will be satisfied.

Franklin L. Kury
Harrisburg, PA

NOTES

1. Lilliard E. Richardson, Jr., David M. Kolinsky, and Jeffrey Milyo, "Public Approval of State Legislatures," *Legislative Studies Quarterly* (Iowa City: Comparative Legislative Research Center, University of Iowa, Feb. 2012), 99-115. Public opinion of the U.S. Congress is much lower. Disapproval of the Congress reached 82 percent in August 2011, according to *The New York Times* (August 4, 2011).

2. David Catanese, "State Polls Show Gathering Storm," POLITICO (March 5, 2010).

3. Listed in Note 11 in Chapter One.

4. See National Conference of State Legislatures (NCSL) website, which provides an overview of legislative term limits and a list of term-limited states. Go to NCSL.org and enter "legislative term limits."

5. Unpublished NCSL document available upon request from the NCSL.

I

Origins and Purposes

Chapter One

The Constitutional Basis

The starting point for evaluating any legislature is the constitution which gave it birth and the constitutional history from which it emerged. The relevant constitutional history began before the states enacted their constitutions and well before the United States became an independent nation. It is worth a few moments to review that pre-American portion of the history as well as the intent of the U.S. Constitution writers following the Revolutionary War. States are part of a federal system and cannot function independent of it. If nothing else, such a review will stir the realization that, regardless of how much reform some may need, state legislatures are a great legacy and deserve our support and appreciation.

THE BEGINNINGS

Almost eight centuries ago an aggressive chief executive confronted an armed rebellion of his major "taxpayers." In resolving the conflict, at least temporarily, this chief executive unwittingly planted the seeds for constitutional government and freely elected legislatures.

The chief executive was King John of England, Ireland and a good piece of northwestern France, who wanted to regain by force of arms portions of France taken from him by the French king. Fighting wars then, as now, was expensive and John looked to barons to provide the support he wanted. He had good reason to expect it. The barons had pledged loyalty to him in exchange for the vast land holdings they held under the feudal system created when William the Conqueror prevailed in his invasion of England a century and a half earlier.

In the spring of 1215 A.D., for a variety of reasons, John found many of the barons in open rebellion. He had to deal with them before he could

Figure 1.1.   King John looks on as his barons sign Magna Carta at Runnymede in June 1215, as imagined by a British artist, c.1850. Source: Bettmann/CORBIS.

resume his re-conquest pursuits in France. After months of intense negotiations and "hard committee work" the King met with the rebels and agreed to a document they had prepared listing a series of grievances against the Crown.[1] The rebellious barons would reaffirm their loyalty to him if he, in exchange, gave them royal assurances that these rights would be upheld. Known as Magna Carta, this document listed over five dozen rights for which the barons wanted a royal guarantee, such as freedom of the church, the liberty of free men, compensation for taking of private property, and procedural rights in criminal cases, as well as a guarantee of the "law of the land."[2]

Of special interest to today's legislators and their constituents is Article 61 of Magna Carta, which provides that the barons would elect from their number a Committee of Twenty-five who would have the authority to review and act upon violations of Magna Carta by the King and his administrators. (The text of Article 61 is in The Legislative Toolbox, "Readings for the Legislative Spirit," in Part Four.) The provision, at least in this author's view, is the first written statement of a legislative check on executive authority. It created the possibility of legislative investigations. This concept developed over several centuries and was transplanted to North America by the British colonial legislatures.

King John had not personally signed Magna Carta and he tried to renege on it.[3] The Royal Seal was, however, affixed to it with his acquiescence, and it was distributed and published throughout the country. That was all that was needed for generations of English barons, lawyers, and politicians to assert over and over again that the English were entitled to civil, legal, and political rights listed in Magna Carta. Through the English Civil War, the Petition of Rights, and the growing strength of the Parliament, an unwritten constitution was created and has been passionately defended.

William Hazeltine, a scholar on the impact of Magna Carta on the American colonies, concluded that

> Rights and liberties of Englishmen embodied in Magna Carta, the [English] Bill of Rights, and other constitutional documents became vital features of colonial constitutional law, and have continued throughout the revolutionary and national epochs to the present day to be essential elements of American constitutional law.[4]

The concept of rights as Englishmen was thus transplanted to the thirteen colonies in the 17th and 18th centuries when colonial legislatures were created to carry out their work under English law. An appointee of the King as Governor often represented the Crown, but the legislators were usually chosen from American-born colonists. Colonial legislatures became robust and were often in conflict with the Crown, which did not hesitate to thwart the legislatures. Legislatures were so important to the Americans of 1776, and the Crown's treatment so resented, they became one of the major reasons Jefferson listed in the Declaration of Independence to justify separation from England. Of twenty-seven grievances listed against George III, five were based on the King's thrashing of the colonial legislatures.

Jefferson wrote of the King's treatment of the colonial legislatures:

> To prove this [the King's absolute tyranny] let Facts be submitted to a candid world....He has refused to pass other Laws for the accommodation of large districts of people, unless those people would relinquish the right of Representation in the legislature, a right inestimable to them and formidable to tyrants only. He has called together legislative bodies at places unusual, uncomfortable, and distant from the depository of their public record, for the sole purpose of fatiguing them into companies with his measures. He has dissolved Representative Houses repeatedly for opposing with manly firmness his invasions of the rights of the people. He has refused for a long time, after such dissolutions, to cause others to be elected, whereby the Legislative powers,

incapable of Annihilation, have returned to the People at large for their exercise.

(The complete text of the Declaration highlighted for the colonial legislatures is in the "Readings for the Legislative Spirit" in the Legislative Toolbox in Part Four.)

Colonial legislatures—to take another metaphor from baseball—became
the spring training grounds for many of the men who would later subscribe to
the Declaration of Independence and write the U.S. Constitution. George
Washington, John Adams, James Madison, and Benjamin Franklin, for example, made their political debuts by running for and being elected to a
colonial legislature.[5] Thus they brought to the writing of the U.S. Constitution great personal knowledge of public affairs gained in their colonial legislatures, as well as their remarkable academic educations. The document they
produced in 1787 combined the best of the British model with the new ideals
of America. This was especially true in regard to replacing the sovereign
monarch with the presidency, an office subject to several checks and bal-
ances. They also decreed that legislatures be a "republican form" of government.

The "republican form" of government contemplated by Madison and his
colleagues is government in which the public grants its power to those
elected by it, but only temporarily. In a direct democracy the citizens themselves vote on public issues.

This is a point of paramount importance. Substantial portions of the Federalist Papers—a series of essays written by Madison, Alexander Hamilton
and John Jay to explain the proposed U.S Constitution—are devoted to explaining and defending this point.[6] Madison feared a direct democracy, be-
lieving that the swirling torrents of volatile public opinion would preclude a
government based on deliberation of issues that should be decided for the
longer view. The plan proposed by Madison and his colleagues was for
Congress and state legislatures of elected solons to deliberate, act and report
to the constituents who chose them. Article IV of the U.S. Constitution
therefore guarantees to every state a republican form of government.

As the states were admitted to the Union following the approval of the
U.S. Constitution, those that had not already enacted a state constitution
adopted their own constitutions, usually modeled after the federal constitution and providing for a republican form of government. The Massachusetts
constitution, written by John Adams in 1781, is the oldest functioning constitution in the world.[7]

At their most fundamental level, constitutions in the United States are
frameworks of government that create three branches—legislative, executive, and judicial. Each state is different. To evaluate the legislature's performance in a particular state it is first necessary to read the constitution for that

Figure 1.2. Portrait of James Madison by Gilbert Stuart, c. 1805. Madison served in the Virginia state legislature and went on to become the leading architect of the American constitutional system. He staunchly advocated the republican form of government. Source: Burstein Collection/CORBIS.

state. The following website gives access to the constitution of each state: www.constitution.org/cons/usstcons.htm.

As you review the constitution for your state, pay particular attention to what the legislature is authorized to do and what the legislature is obligated to do. What rights are guaranteed? In some states the only thing a legislature has to do is enact a budget and means to pay for it. Without that, there can be no government. Everything else is optional with the legislature. But in other states, legislatures are mandated to do more, such as provide for public schooling or preserve wilderness areas.

THE OATH OF OFFICE

No one may serve as a state legislator (or other state official) without taking the oath of office to uphold or support the national and state constitution, regardless of its particulars. The following is the oath in the state of Missouri, a fairly typical example:

> I do solemnly swear, or affirm that I will support the Constitution of the United States and of the state of Missouri, and faithfully perform the duties of my office, and that I will not knowingly receive, directly or indirectly, any money or other valuable thing for the performance or non-performance of any act or duty pertaining to my office, other than the compensation allowed by law.[8]

The oath of office, like a wedding vow, should not be taken lightly. It is not a *pro forma* or ministerial act. It is a commitment to a system of government. What does it mean to take the oath?

Taking the oath signifies a pledge to participate in the government created by the constitution. A legislator is sworn to be part of the government for the whole of the state, not just the district from which he is elected. This is another fundamental point—legislators are responsible for more than their district. They are, along with others, responsible for the government of the entire state.

Since taking the oath is a commitment to participate in a government for the whole state, a question arises. Can a newly elected legislator validly take the oath of office if he has signed previously a written promise never to use or uphold part of the constitution? For example, can one take the oath of commitment to the constitution after having signed the so-called "no tax pledge" of the Americans for Tax Reform? (See Figure 1.3 or go to www.atr.org.)

According to the Americans for Tax Reform website, more than 1,100 state elected officials, legislators and governors have signed its "Taxpayer Protection Pledge." Thirteen Governors were listed as having signed as of February 2012.[9]

There is a constitutional question here. The power to levy taxes is one of the most important provisions of a constitution. There cannot be a government without the assured means of paying for it. To pledge never to increase taxes, under any circumstances, can be construed to say the oath taker is committing to less than the whole of the constitution. Is such a person fully able to carry out their governmental responsibilities?

State Senator Mike Folmer, a conservative Pennsylvania Republican, answered this way:

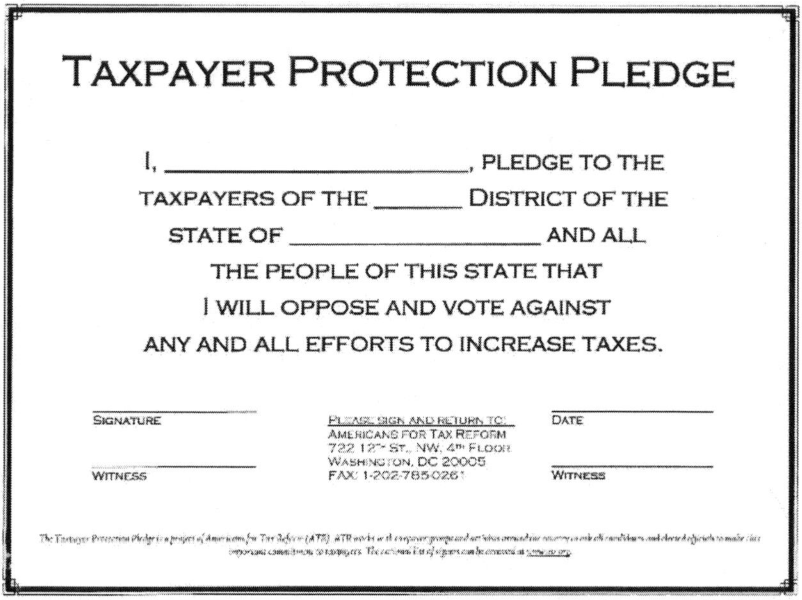

TAXPAYER PROTECTION PLEDGE

I, _____, PLEDGE TO THE

TAXPAYERS OF THE _____ DISTRICT OF THE

STATE OF _____ AND ALL

THE PEOPLE OF THIS STATE THAT

I WILL OPPOSE AND VOTE AGAINST

ANY AND ALL EFFORTS TO INCREASE TAXES.

SIGNATURE _____   PLEASE SIGN AND RETURN TO: DATE _____
                             AMERICANS FOR TAX REFORM
                             722 12ᵀᴴ ST., NW, 4ᵀᴴ FLOOR
                             WASHINGTON, DC 20005
WITNESS _____   FAX: 1-202-785-0261   WITNESS _____

The Taxpayer Protection Pledge is a project of Americans for Tax Reform (ATR). ATR works with taxpayer groups and activists around the country to ask all candidates and elected officials to make this important commitment to taxpayers. The current list of signers can be accessed at www.atr.org.

Figure 1.3.   Taxpayer Protection Pledge advocated by Americans for Tax Reform. Signers of this pledge commit themselves to oppose all tax increases. Source: www.atr.org/.

> …That's why I didn't sign [Grover Norquists's] no-tax [increase] pledge. I'm an anti-tax guy, but I do know we have a constitutional duty, and public transportation is a core role of government and an area we should be spending and fixing. [10]

The oath taking also creates a perpetual opportunity for constituents. They can always ask a legislator his view of a particular provision of the constitution. Most state constitutions have a list of rights guaranteed to their citizens. It is always fair to ask a Representative or Senator what they consider their obligation is to protect, for example, the environmental, equal rights, or right-to-bear-arms provisions in their constitution.

By pledging to carry out the constitution, legislators assume responsibility to be trustees of the historical legacy begun with Magna Carta and so passionately articulated by Thomas Jefferson in the Declaration of Independence. There is no legal authority for this, but I believe it is morally mandated by our own political legacy and the struggles of other countries to develop freely elected legislatures while confronting formidable obstacles. Countries like Iraq, Egypt, Libya and Tunisia—recently liberated from dictatorial regimes—are without the historical background and generations of experience that we in the U.S. were so fortunate to have had when we revolted against King George.

When our colonies achieved independence from England, they were blessed with political leaders like Washington, Adams and Franklin who had considerable experience in legislatures and the resolution of conflict by legislatures. They were ready for self-government.

THE GREAT REBELLION AGAINST
THE REPUBLICAN FORM OF GOVERNMENT

There has been a great rebellion against the republican form of government so strongly advocated by James Madison and guaranteed to every state under Article IV, Sec. IV of the U.S. Constitution. Twenty-four states authorize legislation to be originated and enacted directly by the public [11] under an initiative and referendum process. This "ballot box" method of legislating is deeply ingrained in the body politic of many of the states that allow it, such as California, Oregon, and Colorado.

Initiative and referendum legislating is obviously in direct conflict with the republican form of government advocated by Madison and his colleagues. It came to be because the public in states like California lost confidence that their elected legislators would act in the public interest. Their House and Senate members were seen as under the control of oil companies, insurance companies, mining companies and other special interests. These states decided to take the exclusive power to pass laws out of the hands of the elected. For a good example of why states adopted the initiative and referendum process, see the excerpt on legislative corruption from the Montana Supreme Court opinion in "Readings for the Legislative Spirit" in the Legislative Toolbox, Part Four.

California is of particular interest because it has the largest population of any state and has potentially great political impact on the other 49 states. For the four decades following its admission to the Union, California's government—including both parties in the legislature—was under the solid control of the Southern Pacific Railroad Company and it used that power to maximize its economic position, often at the expense of the public interest. By the early 20th century a new Progressive Party arose to challenge the Southern Pacific machine and its political minions, the Democratic and Republican parties. In 1910, Hiram Johnson, a San Francisco lawyer, in his campaign for Governor traveled over 18,000 miles in an *automobile* to deliver his message—to kick the Southern Pacific machine out of power. Johnson won and California still carries many of the reforms Johnson brought about, such as civil service, child labor laws, and workers' compensation. A major target of Johnson and the Progressive Party was the legislature itself. To deal with its perceived corrupt legislature California enacted the initiative and referendum, or ballot box legislation. But the Johnson reforms also clipped the legislature in another way. As Lou Cannon has reported, the Johnson-Progressive Party legacy included:

> Reduction of the legislative branch of government to a ratifying arm of the executive branch some two decades before the New Deal and America's involvement in global conflict accomplished a similar result federally. Legislatures would retain the power to impede or stymie weak governors, but they would never, until Jesse Unruh came along, initiate their own legislative program independent of the executive. [12]

A century later California's initiative and referendum system is thriving. Consider the scope and complexity of the "ballot box" legislation presented to the voters of California at the 2012 General Election. In addition to voting for President, U.S. Senator, U. S. House members and state legislators, voters were asked to vote on eleven propositions: temporary taxes to fund education; state budget; state and local government; political contributions by payroll deduction; auto insurance prices based on driver history; the death penalty; human trafficking; the three strikes law; genetically engineered foods labeling; tax for education; early childhood programs; business tax for energy funding; and the redistricting of the State Senate.

In the month before the election each household with a registered voter received from the California Secretary of State an official Voter Information Guide of 144 pages, of which 113 pages were devoted to the ballot propositions. Pages 5–11 are a "Quick Reference Guide" to the eleven propositions; pages 12–78 contain an explanation of each proposition, including its background, a legislative analysis, fiscal effects and arguments for and against each one; pages 80–143 provide the text of the statute that will take effect if the proposition is approved. Go to www.voterguide.sos.ca.gov to see the text of the guide. In addition, the advocates and opponents of the propositions spent about $300 million to influence the vote, among the highest to date. [13]

With all of the foregoing, ten million Californians approved four of the propositions (and also the Senate redistricting) and rejected the other six. See the official results at www.vote.sos.ca.gov/returns/ballot-measures.

The late David Broder, one of America's most respected political reporters, closely investigated and analyzed the "initiative and referendum" system in his book, *Democracy Derailed: Initiative Campaigns and the Power of Money*. [14] He concluded that whatever idealism may have led to the instigation of ballot box legislation, it has lost the original intent for the public to originate and enact laws in its own interest. Now, Broder contended, the public is the target of the "initiative and referendum" system, not the originator of its proposals. The reason is simple. To get proposed legislation on the ballot and approved requires a great deal of money to pay for a professional signature collection company to get the required number of names on the petition, to employ lawyers to put the proposal in proper form and get a summary of it approved for the ballot, to hire political strategists to run the campaign, and then to pay for the television and mailings involved. To have a serious chance of success, the proponents of ballot box legislation are limited to those wealthy enough to pay these costs, frequently persons who are speaking for their own interests and many of whom come from out of state.

Broder's conclusion should be sobering for legislators and constituents alike.

> A fundamentally different form of government is not just a possibility; it exists in half the country already…. Do we really wish to keep this a republic? That question is coming at us with the speed of email and with the explosive power of a political bombshell. It is for us and our children to decide what kind of history we want to write. For myself, the choice is easy. I would choose James Madison's design….The remedy to ineffective representation is in our hands each election day. And whatever its flaws, this Republic has consistently provided a government of laws. To discard it for a system that promises laws without government would be a tragic mistake. [15]

In my view, in ballot box legislation, there is no one the public can hold accountable, as it can hold legislators accountable when they are on the ballot personally. The public may know who the major supporters of a referendum question are, but there is no way to make them answer for it politically. The public passes judgment on its legislators every election day.

In ballot box legislation there are no amendments or compromises that are the heart of the "republican" legislative process. On the ballot, it is either "Yes" or "No." In my fourteen years in the legislature, I do not know of a single significant piece of legislation that went to the Governor's desk un-amended. Every major bill I was involved with, such as the public utility code revision and the flood plain management law, took over a dozen amend-ments. Both bills were relatively long and complicated and required exten-sive time in negotiating revisions that would produce enactment. Such revi-sions are impossible under the initiative and referendum system.

But be that as it may, ballot box legislation is not about to recede in its usage. It may even spread. The determining factor will be what the elected Senators and House members do to restore public confidence in the republi-can form of government legislative process.

NOTES

1. Geoffrey Hindley, *A Brief History of Magna Carta: The Story of the Origins of Liberty* (London and Philadelphia: Running Press, 2008), 206.

2. A.E. Dick Howard, *Magna Carta: Text & Commentary* (Charlottesville: University of Virginia Press, 1998), 14–15.

3. Hindley, *A Brief History,* 211.

4. H.D. Hazeltine, *The Influence of Magna Carta on American Constitutional Development* (The Online Library of Liberty), 3.

5. Charles S. Sydor, *American Revolutionaries in the Making* (New York: Colliers Press, 1952).

6. Alexander Hamilton, James Madison, and John Jay, *The Federalist* (New York: Tudor Press, 1947), No. X, XLVIII and XXXIX.

7. David McCullough, *John Adams* (New York: Simon & Schuster, 2001), 220–225.

8. Art. III, Sec. 15 of the Missouri Constitution.

9. www.ATR.org/

10. *Harrisburg Patriot News* interview (August 19, 2013), A13.

11. Massachusetts, Ohio, Michigan, Florida, Mississippi, Arkansas, Missouri, Illinois, Nebraska, North Dakota, South Dakota, Montana, Wyoming, Colorado, Arizona, Utah, Idaho, Washington, Oregon and California.

12. Lou Cannon, *Ronnie & Jesse: A Political Odyssey* (Garden City, NY: Doubleday & Company, 1969), 49. See Chapter Six, "Political Setting" for a good description of California politics originating in the Hiram Johnson era. Much of this paragraph is based on his work.

13. Report of Wyatt Buchanan, *San Francisco Chronicle* (Oct. 21, 2012), 1.

14. David Broder, *Democracy Derailed: Initiative Campaigns and the Power of Money* (Boston: Houghton Mifflin Company, 2005), Chapter 5.

15. Ibid, 243.

Chapter Two

The Work and Nature of Legislatures

The state constitutions lay out the mechanical plans for legislatures—their size, terms, duties, powers and authorizations to be used in their discretion. But the constitutions do not put vitality into legislatures. Vitality comes from the people who elect legislators and serve in them. Legislatures are not designed to be judged by notions of mechanical efficiency, but—hopefully—by the manner in which they act on public issues in a reasoned and timely fashion. To understand how they work it is appropriate to look at the work of legislatures and examine how human nature comes into play on the constitutional structure.

THE WORK OF LEGISLATURES

The work of legislatures has three parts—lawmaking, enacting a budget and the means to pay for it, and oversight through investigations and questions.

Lawmaking

Lawmaking is the role citizens generally associate with legislatures. Most people have a fundamental idea of the legislative process—the introduction of a bill, its consideration by a committee, and passage on the floor, then to the other chamber and finally the Governor.

Each state has its own idiosyncrasies in the lawmaking process. To understand fully the procedure in your state, go the home page website for your legislature. Most, if not all, have a segment describing in detail its legislative process. For example, the State of Washington's legislative website has "An Overview of the Legislative Process."[1]

Michigan's website has an information program, which includes "The Legislative Process," complete with a section "Helpful Hints for Contacting Your State Legislator."[2]

The lawmaking authority of legislatures is far more sweeping than is generally understood. Limited only by the state and U.S. constitutions, legislatures have jurisdiction over subjects ranging from marriage and reproductive rights to who shall receive the death penalty.

Laws enacted by state legislatures also govern all elections, state, local and federal. Nothing is more important to our political system than voting. Yet, state and local officials conduct all elections. Voter identification, early voting, absentee voting, and voter registration are all subject to some federal requirements, enacted and implemented by state and local, not federal, officials. In the year 2000 the outcome of the Presidential election was decided by how the U.S. Supreme Court looked at Florida's election law.[3] In short, the lawmaking power of state legislatures is awesome and not to be underappreciated.

Budgets and Taxes

Passing a state budget and providing the funds to pay for it is a special section of the lawmaking power that is perhaps more important than the rest. Without a budget there can be no government to implement the laws enacted. Most of the other lawmaking is discretionary, that is, not mandated as is the budget.

The normal process is for the Governor to propose a budget for a single year or for two years. The legislature must then pass the budget and the taxes to pay for it. The Governor proposes the budget and any taxes needed for funding, but only the legislature can enact the budget and taxes. This division of power between the executive and legislative branches is a fundamental check and balance that goes to the heart of our constitutional system. Neither the executive nor the legislature can provide for the operation of a government on its own.

The power to pass budgets and levy taxes is the most important single power a legislature has. Around this power is the great issue facing America's political parties today—what is the proper size and role of government?

King John found that he could not raise enough revenue to fund his war in France without the agreement of his Lords, who in turn demanded something in return, as stated in Magna Carta. The conflict between governors and lawmakers has continued for eight centuries, but is now done through peaceful and civil negotiations.

Investigations and Questioning

Hidden within the seemingly lethargic legislative institutions are great powers to investigate, inquire, recommend and then act. When this power is well used, the legislatures produce outstanding results in the public interest. Starting with the Committee of Twenty-Five Barons authorized by Magna Carta to report on violations of the charter by the King's administration, legislatures have developed the power to investigate and question how public funds are spent, as well as the conditions that are subject to the "police power" the state government has to protect lives and property.

The classic illustration of this latent power came in New York State in 1911 following the Triangle Shirtwaist Factory fire in which 146 workers were killed, many jumping from windows because the doors to their factory opened in, not out, and were locked. The public reaction was strong. The New York state legislature, through its leaders Robert Wagner and Alfred Smith, created a Factory Investigation Commission that they personally led. The Commission held 59 public hearings, heard 472 witnesses, and (through the committee staff) visited 3,385 workplaces. The Commission recommended 17 legislative bills and 13 of them were passed. New York factories and related workplaces became much safer. [4]

Legislatures do not need such dramatic events as the Triangle Shirtwaist fire to do salutary investigative or inquiry work. While in the Pennsylvania Senate, I chaired a committee that investigated the Pennsylvania's Public Utility Commission, an agency created by the legislature 35 years earlier and never looked at thereafter. We held six hearings, heard 25 witnesses from every section of the utility community, took field trips to California and Wisconsin, and produced a report that led to a greatly revised commission and the creation of a consumer advocate. [5]

Every legislature has examples of legislative investigations and reviews that produced comparable or better results. My impression, however, is that the legislatures do not use this investigative power often or regularly enough, especially in light of the substantially increased size of the staff they now have. Legislators are so involved with day-to-day struggles and conflicts that they do not take the time or make the effort to take a longer view. Legislators and constituents alike can ask of their legislature: How does it use its power to investigate? What agencies or programs need a legislative review?

THE NATURE OF LEGISLATURES

Large Committees at Work

To run for the legislature is to seek the most challenging "committee work" there is. Legislatures are really large committees. There are two in each state except Nebraska, and it takes collective action of the members—at least a majority of each chamber—to act. The smallest bicameral legislature is Alaska with 60 (40 House and 20 Senate) and the largest is New Hampshire with 424 (400 House and 24 Senate).[6] Wherever they rank in the range of size, legislatures are subject to the forces of leadership, deference, confidence, fear, candor and deception that are found in committees of a church, P.T.A., or other civic organizations. For legislatures, these forces are magnified by the potentially explosive nature of the issues to be acted upon. Add to this the great pressures of lobbyists and other interested advocates and the legislatures as institutions become restrained in how quickly they can act.

Compromise is a Staple of Legislative Vitality

Because legislatures are in effect large committees, compromise is a staple of their function. Without it the legislative process is frozen in dysfunction, as is demonstrated by the ongoing stalemate in the U.S. Congress between the House, Senate, and White House. Every legislator is sworn to govern for the entire state and therefore must consider the importance of yielding his position for the good of the whole. Anyone, legislator or constituent, who doubts this fact, should revisit the U.S. Constitution and how it was written.

Catherine Drinker Bowen tells that story well in *Miracle at Philadelphia*.[7] For four months, May through September of 1787, the delegates to the Constitutional Convention argued, deliberated, and compromised through a series of contentious issues such as how small states and large states should be represented, the powers to be given the President, the length of terms for the House and Senate, and slavery. The final document, our Constitution, was a series of compromises.

Men of very differing views gave in or otherwise made adjustments because of a desire to create a government all of them could support. Not all of the delegates agreed, but enough did to make it happen. British Prime Minister Gladstone, in 1887, called the U.S. Constitution the "most remarkable work known to me in modern times to have been produced by the human intellect."[8] It would not have happened without compromise, lots of it. A House elected for two years based on population and Senators appointed by state legislatures for six years and Senatorial confirmation of Presidential nominations are two examples of the compromises in the U.S. Constitution.

Compromise requires a common ground on which contending parties can meet in spite of their differences. In the case of the U.S. Constitution, the common ground was the desire to create a new frame of government that, unlike the Articles of Confederation, would function effectively. In the case of state legislatures in contemporary times the common ground must be to carry out their constitutional mandate to run a government.

Reactive Bodies

Legislatures are generally reactive bodies, seemingly plodding in pace, unless prompted to act by strong leadership, a constitutional deadline or a dramatic event. A flash of public outrage, however, can prompt surprisingly quick action, especially on the introduction of bills. In July 2011 a Florida jury failed to convict the mother of a child discovered thirty days after her unreported death. The verdict in the Casey Anthony trial ignited such public consternation that legislatures in twelve states quickly introduced bills to make it a felony for parents to fail to report the death or disappearance of a child.[9]

There are numerous similar cases where legislation is sparked by a public outcry. Perhaps the most famous is Megan's Law requiring convicted sex offenders to register their presence wherever they reside. This law was rapidly passed state after state following the rape and murder of Megan Kanka, a seven year old, by a previously unknown sex offender who lived near her in New Jersey. On May 17, 1996, President Clinton signed a federal Megan's Law.[10]

Conflict and Controversy

The normal atmosphere in which legislatures function is constantly shrouded in clouds of controversy—gun rights, gay rights, animal rights, environmental rights and more. Many voters are put off by constant conflict over such issues, and that is unfortunate. Constituents need to understand that legislatures will always be forums confronting emotional issues. To expect otherwise is to expect what will never be. David Leopold, a writer for *POLITICO*, put it bluntly:

> ... Conflict is unavoidable in our system. It was designed to foster conflict (e.g., the separation of powers) and many of the recent developments in the system (e.g., the omnipresent media) only exacerbate it; conflict is an inevitable part of politics and politics, in turn, is essential to a healthy democracy and a free society. The governing process is complex and simplistic demands that elected officials put aside their principles, not to mention the interests they represent, and "get something" done are silly at best and counterproductive at worst. Indeed democracy cannot function properly with a public that doesn't have the stomach for politics and doesn't understand it well enough to engage in it constructively.[11]

The presence of conflict in legislative forums is not, then, a cause of concern. The question is not whether there will be conflict, but how it will be resolved. If our states cannot resolve emotional issues in a legislature, how will it be done? By ballot box legislation that is dominated by the wealthy interests, as discussed in Chapter One? By violence or force of arms? The question should have been settled by King John and the Barons of England in 1215.

Whatever their faults, elected legislatures are still the best system. The alternatives are worse. Only elected legislatures provide for the wielding of governmental power in a manner that is regularly subject to public approval and are close enough to the public to feel its opinions.

Individual Legislators

A principal qualification for effective legislative membership is the ability to have an amicable relationship with those who hold substantially differing views. To succeed and have a sense of satisfaction under the conditions just described, a member, while having strong feelings on issues, recognizes that everyone else in the chamber may also have strong feelings and many of them will be different. Integral to this point is the willingness to listen and to consider different points of view. Absent these attributes, an aspiring legislator really ought to seek a different line of work.

Madison and his colleagues contemplated legislatures where the members would deliberate on issues in a civil manner, even when the issue was contentious and the debate pointed. A fundamental principle flows from this: Legislators must be free to use their judgment, not just reflect public opinion.

The classic statement of this is found in Edmund Burke's Bristol Constituency speech of 1774:

> It ought to be the happiness and glory of a representative to live in the strictest union, the closest correspondence, and the most unreserved communication with his constituents. Their wishes ought to have great weight with him; their opinion high respect; their business unremitted attention. It is his duty to sacrifice his repose, his pleasures, his satisfaction, to theirs; and above all, even, and in all cases, to prefer their interest to his own. *Your representative owes you, not his industry only, but his judgment; and he betrays instead of serving you if he sacrifices it to your opinion.* (Emphasis added.) [12]

Burke's point goes to the central question of what an individual member is to do. Is it just to represent the opinion of his district, or it is something more?

The question has arisen in Pennsylvania where Majority Party PA, a political action committee of citizens, has asked legislative candidates to sign the Candidate Public Service Pledge (see Figure 2.1).

If a legislator signs this pledge, he or she is in direct conflict with Edmund Burke's plea that the legislator owes his constituents his judgment, even if it is contrary to their opinion. How far does this pledge commit legislators to be controlled by public opinion polls? If there are public opinion research facilities that accurately measure public opinion, how much longer do we need to elect legislators? Why not do it all by direct electronic

2012 Candidate Public Service Pledge

I, (name as it appears on the ballot) _____candidate for (office)

See the Majority Party PA website for information on its origins and goals, why the majority party type people pledge to be a public servant putting the priorities of the people I represent ahead of my own.

I pledge to make decisions and cast votes affecting the citizens of the Commonwealth that reflect the will of the majority of PA citizens as publicly documented by scientific public opinion research.

Signature:_____ Date:_____

Witness:_____ Date:_____

Witness:_____ Date:_____

In 2012, the Majority Party PA is asking candidates for the legislature to sign this.

Those who do will be listed under the "Public Servants" tab on our home page. Those who do not will be listed under the "Public Masters" list.

Figure 2.1.   2012 Candidate Public Service Pledge proposed by Majority Party PA, a legislative reform group in Harrisburg, PA. Source: www.themajoritypartypa.com/.

democracy and have everyone vote with his or her computer? There is one other flaw in this pledge. As valid as public opinion research can be, it is a like a weather report—good for the next hour. Madison and others have warned of the vagaries of public opinion and the dangers of relying on it for permanent policy. Public opinion polls are not solid ground on which to build public structures.

Figure 2.2.   New Jersey state senators consider a gun control measure on April 30, 2013, as Trenton Senator Nia Gill speaks, while Senators Stephen Sweeney and Loretta Weinberg look on. Source: Julio Cortez/AP/CORBIS.

If all the individual legislator does is reflect the public opinion of his district, why do we need legislatures? In today's world of sophisticated electronics, citizens voting through their computers could easily resolve every legislative issue.[13] But that would not allow for focused evaluation and amendments. How can an entire state be governed if each elected legislator merely votes the polling in his district? That could be condemnation to permanent stalemate. Electronic wizardry cannot substitute for human judgment or negotiation.

NOTES

1. www.leg.wa.gov/legislature/Pages/Overview.aspx.

2. www.legislature.mi.gov/documents/publications/forthepeople.pdf.

3. *Bush v. Gore*, 531 U.S. 98 (2000).

4. Arthur M. Schlesinger, Jr., *The Crisis of the Old Order* (Boston: Houghton Mifflin Company, 1957), 96. Also, the U.S. Dept. of Labor—History website.

5. Franklin L. Kury, *Clean Politics, Clean Streams* (Bethlehem, PA: Lehigh University Press, 2011), 106–120.

6. NCSL website. Number of State Legislators and Length of Terms (in years).

7. Catherine Drinker Bowen, *Miracle at Philadelphia* (Boston: Little Brown Company, 1966).

8. John Bartlett, *Familiar Quotations* (Boston: Little, Brown & Co., 1955), 534.

9. Robbie Brown, *The New York Times*, (July 9, 2011), A14.

10. See the Klaas Kids Foundation website (www.klaaskids.org/pg-legmeg.htm/) for the status of Megan's Law in each of the 50 states.

11. David Leopold, "Get Over It— Political Conflict Is Unavoidable." *POLITICO* (August 2, 2011).

12. Bartlett, *Quotations*, 359.

13. See Alan Rosenthal, *Decline in Representative Democracy* (Washington, DC: CQ Press, 1998), 38– 39, for a discussion of electronic democracy.

II

Sources of Discontent

Chapter Three

Private Benefits versus Public Service

COMPENSATION: SALARIES, EXPENSES AND PENSIONS

On July 7, 2005, the Pennsylvania General Assembly voted to raise its pay by 16 percent ($11,403), from $69,647 to $81,050 for rank-and-file members and 34 percent for the leadership. The formal increase would not take place until after the next election, but the members could start collecting it immediately as "un-vouchered expenses." There had been no hearings or prior public discussion of this legislation. The Senate Republican leadership, the House Democratic leadership, and Governor Rendell agreed to it and it became law—for a short while. Public outrage was strong and swift.[1] The next day a large, rubber "pink pig" occupied the steps of the state capitol. The law was repealed on November 5, 2005, and the Senate leaders of the effort went down in defeat in the next primary election. Many legislators chose voluntary retirement rather than face voters at the next election. The November 2006 election for the General Assembly produced the largest freshman class in years.

Ironically an argument could have been made to justify the increase. Many legislators earn it by long hours and hard work on a state government with a budget of more than $25 billion. By not laying out the justification before the vote, the legislators forfeited their chances to do so afterward. The public was so angry that no one would listen. The Pennsylvania legislature had overlooked a fundamental rule: legislators serve as agents of their constituencies and need public approval for their compensation. Public approval is traditionally sought by providing that a salary increase will not take effect until after the next legislative election. This was an important principle of the U. S. Constitution writers, as shown in the 27th Amendment proposed in 1791 (and finally adopted in 1992!).[2] It reads: "No law varying the compen-

Figure 3.1.   The Pink Pig that appeared on the steps of Pennsylvania's capitol shortly after the midnight legislative pay raise of 2005. Source: Franklin Kury.

sation for the services of the Senators and Representatives shall take effect, until an election of Representatives shall have intervened."

Many state constitutions contain similar provisions. This principle assures that the benefiting legislators stand accountable for their actions in approving the increase.

Some defenders of the 2005 pay increase say that to do it any other way would mean that there would be no increases. This may be true, especially in states, like Pennsylvania, where legislative compensation far exceeds the income of the average family. But that goes with the territory, so to speak. Representatives and Senators are in the public service. All are "volunteers." None are appointed, drafted or conscripted for the work. Although it varies from state to state, the typical term for Representatives is still two years and for Senators four.

Legislative salaries and how they are enacted are important factors in determining public opinion of the legislature. There is a wide diversity in the amount of salaries and how they are determined. Seven states have no fixed salary, but compensate with a per diem payment for each day in session. In 2012 Kansas, for example, paid $88.66 per day for a 90-day session, producing an effective salary of $7,979.40. Seven states have salaries over $50,000, with California being the highest at $95,291. New Mexico provides no salary at all, only per diem expenses. For a complete list of the states and the salary and expense payments for legislators, go to the Empire Center website: www.empirecenter.org/html/legislative_salaries.cfm.

While there are websites showing what legislative salaries are, there is no website showing how they are set in each state. The National Conference of State Legislators (NCSL), however, has an unpublished list with this information which it will share with anyone who requests a copy.[3]

Pennsylvania, along with Iowa, Missouri, New York, Virginia, and New Jersey, is among the states where the legislature is the final authority on setting its salary. In Arizona and Texas, the voters at the ballot box must approve salaries. In three states, Washington, Michigan and California, an independent commission sets the salaries. Florida, Massachusetts, North Carolina, Wisconsin and Georgia correlate legislative salaries to state employees' salaries.[4]

Pensions

In judging legislative compensation, however, the salary and expense allowances are like that portion of an iceberg above the water line. Often times a larger element of compensation is pension benefits, which in many cases far exceed the size of the formal salary on which they are based.

Pension benefits for legislators have not traditionally been readily available, although they are now becoming more so. While salaries and expenses are now available to anyone through a single website, there is nothing comparable yet available to the public on pensions. The legislative financial offices usually consider pension information private and legislators are reluctant to discuss the subject. The startling amounts of some benefits have been disclosed only when the legislator retired.

Obtaining information on legislative pension systems has until recently required a substantial effort, like getting a good picture of the ice under the water line of an iceberg. The newspaper *USA TODAY* made such an effort by reviewing thousands of pages of law from the 40 states that provide legislative pensions[5] to find out how legislative pensions are determined.

Thomas Frank, the reporter, published the results of the *USA TODAY* investigation on November 12, 2011. The story revealed some state pension systems replete with egregious examples of strikingly high benefits determined by obscure ways of calculating the final pension. See the USA TODAY website.www.usatoday.com/news/nation/2011-11-1A-state-lawmakers-pump-pensions.htm.

As reported by Frank, some legislatures have been ingenious in finding ways to increase their pensions. Most pensions, public or private, are determined by a percentage of salary multiplied by years of service and the reaching of a certain age. Some have defined the normal salary to include expenses and per diems received. Other states allow serving legislators to receive their pensions while still serving in the legislature, a practice called "double-dipping." Some allow legislators to collect their pension after only five or ten years of service.

According to the *USA TODAY* report, 570 legislators in nineteen states qualify for pensions that will pay them as much or more—in one case seventeen times more—than they are now receiving as salary. In short, some legislatures have created a system that gives some senior legislators unique special benefits, well beyond those in the regular state employ or private business, an indication that confirms the public view that legislators are in it more for themselves than for the public.

The NCSL has compiled an unpublished table of how legislative pensions are determined for those elected after 2002 and 2003. This table shows that legislatures are taking action to reform the egregious pension benefits that detract from the public estimation of the legislatures. As of February 2010 California eliminated pensions for legislators elected after 1990, Louisiana for those elected after 1997, and Rhode Island for those elected after 1995.[6]

The 2005 pay-raise disaster in Pennsylvania and the USA TODAY story on pensions are a stark background for the dilemmas facing modern legislatures. How can legislators be properly compensated while still maintaining public confidence? How much longer will legislatures support a pension system that is heavily veiled from public view? Can the legislative pension system be brought into conformity with a concept of public service and be fair to legislators who have abandoned other careers for an uncertain future in elected public office?

Is it fair not to allow legislators, particularly in the larger states where there they are "full-time," to participate in a pension program? Can legislators be effective leaders for the public if the impression they give is that they serve in order to receive substantial personal benefits?

There are two elements to resolving these questions. First, states must make the legislative pension system consistent with public service, providing fair compensation based on a system that is fully disclosed. The other is that changes made by legislatures should not take place until after the next election, a principle provided in some state constitutions as well as in the 27th Amendment to the U.S. Constitution.

THE RISE OF THE FULL-TIME LEGISLATURE

There is a second dilemma confronting the states with "professional" legislatures, that is, legislatures where the members and staff are paid to devote their efforts solely to legislative service and without outside work. How do such legislatures insure that they stay true to the purpose for which they were created?

In 1969, my third year in the Pennsylvania House, Herbert Fineman, the newly elected Speaker, spoke to our caucus about his plans to modernize the legislature: "How can this legislature effectively evaluate the Governor's budget requests when we have so little capacity to do it? We have virtually no staff and no research capability. If we are to be a co-equal branch of state government we need to arm ourselves for the job."

Fineman's argument made sense to me. When I arrived in the House in January 1967 I was given no seat, except the seat on the floor of the House, no office, staff, or telephone. The salary was $7200 a year. The committees I served on had no staffing except a secretary. Yet my colleagues and I were expected to pass independent judgment on a $3 billion budget prepared over six months by the Governor's staff with the support of all of the executive branch agencies.

I recall one of my House colleagues, Joseph Kolter, asking Charles McIntosh, the Governor's budget secretary, "Where can we cut this budget?" "I can't tell you that," McIntosh replied. "My job is to draft the budget. You [the legislature] have to take it from there."

Fineman, with the support of the Republican leadership, initiated 13 new procedural changes in the House that launched it on the way becoming an "equal coordinate branch."[7] These changes included professional committee staffing, preparation of fiscal notes on bills involving expenditures of state funds, and increased use of public hearings.

At the same time, on the West Coast, California House Speaker Jesse Unruh had begun to implement parallel plans for his legislature. In 1966 he had, working with the Republican leadership, engineered public approval of referendum Proposition 1-A that changed the California constitution to authorize legislative pay raises without a popular vote and to make the legislature a "full-time" position. With that referendum approved, Unruh and other legislative leaders expanded staffing and obtained expertise on finance and related issues not previously available. A new legislative system was created and legislative policymaking began to flourish.[8]

Unruh's efforts were so impressive that Lou Cannon, who studied California politics closely for decades, put it this way:

> Unruh's attempt to provide the California Legislature with decision-making capability of its own must be rated one of the most significant modern experiments in American government. The experiment is at once forward-looking and conservative, for it seeks both to provide the Legislature with the capability to deal with the nation's mounting social ills and at the same time to restore the independence of a steadily deteriorating branch of government revered by the Founding Fathers as the wellspring of democracy.[9]

In the decades since Fineman and Unruh launched the full-time legislative programs, both legislatures have changed immensely. In 2012 in Califor-

Figure 3.2.   California House Speaker Jesse Unruh shakes hands with Governor Ronald Regan, with Mrs. Reagan on the left, at the Capitol in Sacramento, 1967. Reagan supported Unruh's ballot box initiative to create a modern legislature. Source: Bettmann/CORBIS.

nia, legislators were paid $95,290.56 a year and also $141.86 per day in session and given a state car. In Pennsylvania the salary was $79,613 plus actual expenses or a per diem and a car.

The California legislative staff grew from 1,760 in 1979 to 2,106 in 2009. Pennsylvania's staffing grew from 1,430 in 1979 to 2,919 in 2009, making it the largest legislative staff in the country. The total staffing for all state legislatures grew from 16,939 in 1979, to 26,972 in 1996, to about 35,000 today.[10]

The increase in the size of legislative staffing is not, in itself, grounds for objecting to it. The question is what does the public get for the larger staffing? What does a legislature do with its staff?

Somewhere along the way the concept of a full-time legislature supported by a professional staff went off the tracks in at least two states. California and Pennsylvania developed complications that produced results unexpected by Unruh and Fineman. The compensation package for service in both legislatures grew to the point that it became a reason for seeking election and re-election. This raised an important question. What was the reason a legislator sought re-election—to further the public interest or to protect his or her financial interest? Both? Which comes first on tough issues?

The need for campaign funding further aggravated the problem. The cost of campaigns for state legislative seats escalated immensely. In my first campaign in 1966 I defeated the senior Republican in the House with $7500 of my (and my wife's) money and a platoon of volunteers who hand-addressed 18,000 envelopes and made hundreds of telephone calls. Now a typical winning campaign for the House in Pennsylvania costs about $200,000. As will be discussed in Chapter Three, the costs in other states have risen comparably.

Control of a legislative house in a major state demands extraordinary expenditures not contemplated when the legislative modernization efforts began. As a result the leadership in a large legislature can be tempted to use their enlarged legislative staff for political purposes. In California, the professional legislative staff contemplated by Unruh transformed into a squad of campaign workers for the legislative leaders. The staff shifted from being a professional adjunct of the legislators to taxpayer-funded political muscle.[11]

The same affliction came to Pennsylvania, where in 2008 and 2009 twenty-five former House members and staff were charged with the crime of using public funds for campaign purposes in a series of trials known as "Bonusgate." They had used public funds to give bonuses to legislative staff for work on legislative campaigns. Two were acquitted and the charges dropped on one, but the twenty-three convicted or who pled guilty included two former House Speakers and their top staff.[12]

Is it any wonder that the legislatures of California and Pennsylvania have such a high negative public opinion? In their study of the public approval of state legislatures, Lilliard Richardson and his colleagues at the University of Iowa Legislative Research Center reported:

> Legislative approval is surprisingly low in states with highly professionalized legislatures, such as California, Michigan, and New York, and higher in states with citizen legislatures, such as North Dakota, Utah and Wyoming....[There is] a negative correlation between legislative professionalism and public approval.[13]

There is a great irony in this. A major reason for hiring professional legislative staff is to enable the legislatures to be co-equal branches of government with the governors. In Pennsylvania, at least, this goal has been reached. The Pennsylvania legislature has enacted and the Governor signed a budget bill for 2012-2013 that was the result of weeks of negotiations between the Governor and the leaders of the House and Senate, even though all of them are Republican. Is the legislature co-equal to the Governor? The final budget contains appropriations of $517 million more than the Governor wanted.

A question for readers: Is the size of staffing in your legislature justified? The number of legislative employees may have grown exponentially, but the number of legislators has not.

The answers depend on what each legislature does with its staffing, how it is directed by the members. If the staffing is used to help the members understand increasingly complex issues, service constituents, process legislation and exercise the legislature's latent power to investigate and recommend changes, the staffing is justified. To the extent it is used for something else, like campaign purposes, it is not. What is the situation in your state?

NOTES

1. Associated Press report of August 10, 2005.
2. Wikipedia website for the 27th Amendment to the U.S. Constitution.
3. National Conference of State Legislatures, 7700 East First Place, Denver, CO, 80230. (303) 354–7700.
4. Memo of Melissa S. Cate, Illinois General Assembly Legislative Unit, Sept. 4, 2008, from the Illinois General Assembly website and the NCSL list.
5. Seven States do not provide legislative pensions—Alabama, Nebraska, New Hampshire, North Dakota, South Dakota, Vermont and Wyoming. Four states do not allow pensions for those elected after a cut-off date, the most recent of which is 1999. These states are California, Arkansas, Louisiana, and Rhode Island. See NCSL list.
6. State Retirement Provisions for State Legislatures, NCSL, March 2010.
7. Herbert Fineman, "Looking Back at the Legislative Modernization Movement," *Commonwealth: A Journal of Political Science*, Vol.1254 (2003), 87–110. The author, along with Representative K. Leroy Irvis, was the sponsor of the fiscal note requirement for every bill involving the expenditure of funds. In 1977 Fineman was convicted on two counts of obstruction of justice in connection with placements to graduate schools. *U.S. vs. Fineman*, U.S. Court for the Eastern District of PA (1977). In the author's view, this does not detract from the legislative reform work that he led.
8. Bill Boyarsky, *Big Daddy: Jesse Unruh and the Art of Power Politics* (Los Angeles: University of California, 2008), 164.
9. Lou Cannon, *Ronnie and Jesse: A Political Odyssey* (Garden City, NY: Doubleday and Co., 1969), 208.
10. Alan Rosenthal, et al., *Republic on Trial: The Case for Representative Democracy* (Washington, DC: CQ Press, 2003), 179–180.
11. Boyarsky, *Big Daddy, 169.*
12. *Harrisburg Patriot*, June 28, 2012, A-3 and 4. See also Chapter 12 of Brad Bumsted's *Keystone Corruption*, included in the Bibliography in the Legislative Toolbox, for a detailed account of Bonusgate.
13. Lilliard E. Richardson, Jr., et al., "Public Approval of State Legislatures," *Legislative Studies Quarterly* (Iowa City: Comparative Legislative Research Center, University of Iowa, Feb. 2012), 4.

Chapter Four

Scandal and Ethical Questions

When I came to the Senate of Pennsylvania in 1973 Senator Frank Mazzei was a prominent member of the Democratic majority. A legislative veteran, he provided the drive to enact the state's lottery law and had aspirations to be the majority leader. In November of 1974, however, a federal jury in the Western District of Pennsylvania found Mazzei guilty under the federal anti-racketeering law of extorting money from state leaseholders, a criminal offense that barred him forever from serving in the state legislative seat or any other public office.

The Senate Republican minority promptly called for Mazzei's resignation but he declined. Lieutenant Governor Ernest Kline provided an opinion from the Legislative Reference Bureau that, although the jury had found Mazzei guilty, he had not yet been convicted. There was, the ruling said, no conviction until Mazzei was sentenced. The court sentenced Mazzei in May of 1975 and he still did not resign. The Republican minority again called for his resignation or expulsion. Mazzei argued that he was entitled to an appeal before the Senate acted, and the Democratic leadership was inclined to support Mazzei, one of their own. As a freshman Democrat I did the same. But one Democratic Senator, Joseph Ammerman, was not satisfied. Ammerman had been the U. S. Attorney for Western Pennsylvania before his election to the Senate. He contacted his former office, obtained a copy of the transcript of the Mazzei trial and shared it with the Senate Democratic leadership and others, including me. After reading it, the Democratic leadership concluded that they had no choice but to expel Mazzei regardless of the appeal. I agreed. Consequently, on June 2, 1975 the Senate voted 49–0 to expel Frank Mazzei. He is the only Senator ever expelled from office in Pennsylvania history.

In retrospect, the Mazzei case is clear. A Senator had been convicted of a felony and under Pennsylvania's Constitution had to go.[1] It took a little while, but the Senate Democratic leadership did what any legislative leadership should do in such cases, regardless of how popular or powerful the transgressor may be. The Senate set a precedent for the principle that a conviction is a conviction upon sentencing. But the Senate also provided a key test for legislatures everywhere—how decisively does it act on such matters?

Scandals like Mazzei's still occur throughout the fifty legislatures. In the eighteen months from January 2011 through June 2012, legislators in Arizona, Georgia, Illinois, New York, Alabama, and Pennsylvania left office because of bribery or misuse of public funds. South Carolina, Texas, California, Florida and Maine saw legislators leave for lesser charges.[2]

These scandals must be kept in perspective. They involve only a small handful of the 7,382 people serving as legislators and their transgressions should not tarnish public opinion of the others. The inescapable fact is that there will always be such scandals in legislatures, just as there will always be comparable scandals in churches, banks, sports, and universities. Human nature makes it impossible to have a group of 7,328 that does not reflect the range of moral values of the society from which it is elected. Crimes will occur. The question for a legislature is what it will do with those who violate the law when it learns this has happened.

The overwhelming majority of legislators who are convicted of a crime resign promptly after conviction or have left office beforehand. However, as the Mazzei case illustrates, the legislature must be ready to act and act decisively.

Far more common problems likely to confront legislators are ethical questions on issues like receiving gifts and hospitality from lobbyists, personal financial disclosure, conflict of interest and use of public resources for political campaign purposes. These questions go to the integrity of each legislative chamber. Most ethical problems are found in shades of gray, not in the black-and-white clarity of criminal law violations such as Mazzei's.

As legislatures are independent branches of government, they and they alone have the power to seat, discipline and expel members. Courts and ethics commissions may find legislators guilty of misconduct and impose penalties, but expulsion is not one of those penalties. Only a House or Senate can expel a member.

This fundamental rule of constitutional law places the initial responsibility on legislatures to maintain their institutional integrity by enacting and enforcing rules of ethical conduct. The initial and primary responsibility to do this rests with each legislative chamber. To the extent that legislative bodies do not carry out the responsibility of overseeing the conduct of their members, others, such as state ethics commissions, will.

What are the potential consequences for a legislature when the "outside" ethics enforcers take over because the legislature has failed to do what it ought to have done? Consider the recent sexual harassment case in the New York Assembly (the House of Representatives in most states).

On August 26, 2012, *The New York Times* carried the headline "Assemblyman Censured Over Charges of Sexually Harassing Two Employees." The story, written by Danny Hakim, reported that the Speaker of the Assembly, Sheldon Silver, had stripped Assemblyman Vito J. Lopez of his committee chairmanship and censured him for allegedly sexually assaulting two female employees. The Speaker said he decided to censure Mr. Lopez after the Assembly's ethics committee—four Democrats and four Republicans—ruled unanimously that there was credible evidence that Lopez had verbally and physically harassed the employees.

At first blush, the New York Assembly seemed to be doing what it should do—taking action to clean its own house. Unfortunately there was much more. On August 26, 2012, *The New York Times* carried another headline, "Before Censure, a Hushed Settlement Against Assemblyman," in which Hakim and Thomas Kaplan reported that Speaker Silver had settled other accusations against Lopez before censuring him. In this and later stories the *Times* reported that Silver had agreed to pay $103,000 of public funds to women in other sexual harassment complaints against Lopez that were not reported to the Assembly ethics' committee. From there the case, which was one the Assembly could and should have handled internally, spun rapidly out of its hands.

The Assembly Speaker admitted that he had erred in secretly agreeing to the settlements. The outrage against the Speaker quickly surpassed that against Assemblyman Lopez.

On August 27, 2012, the *New York Times* editorialized,

> The Lopez case begs for a more thorough investigation by those outside the legislative cocoon....The new Joint Commission on Public Ethics as well as the local Albany prosecutor should each be opening a file on Mr. Lopez....Mr. Silver's confidential settlement arrangement also demands a closer look.

The New York State Joint Commission on Public Ethics (JCOPE) is a bipartisan Commission of fourteen members, none of whom are legislators, that has jurisdiction over both executive and legislative ethics. JCOPE commenced an investigation that included issuing 49 subpoenas, interviewing more than 45 witnesses, and reviewing more than 20,000 documents. On February 12, 2013 JCOPE issued a report that concluded,

> ...There is a substantial basis to conclude that Lopez used his office to pursue a course of conduct that was in violation of the public trust, to secure unwarranted benefits, and to give a reasonable basis for the impression one could

unduly enjoy his favor in performance of one's official duties…that Lopez
violated the Public Officials Law… through knowing and intentional conduct…."

The Speaker eventually said he would seek expulsion of Lopez from the
House. Lopez resigned before that could happen and sought to rehabilitate
his political career by seeking election to the New York City Council. Lopez
was soundly defeated in that election.

Lopez's personal public career disintegrated in a ball of fire and the New
York General Assembly itself has been damaged. JCOPE found that the
Speaker of the House and his staff shielded Lopez. In a poll reported by *The
New York Times* on June 5, 2013, New York voters by a two-to-one margin
wanted the Speaker to resign. Speaker Silver is still in office, but stuck in a
quagmire of litigation and public dissatisfaction with the way he handled the
matter. [3]

**Figure 4.1.   Governor Andrew Cuomo of New York announced, on July 13, 2013,
a commission to investigate the State Board of Elections and fundraising among
state legislators. Source: Mike Groll/AP/CORBIS.**

There are likely to be more developments in the Lopez and Silver matters. In the meanwhile the question recurs for every legislature in the United States. Could your House and Senate handle cases like the Lopez case with a full investigation, complete transparency to the public, and firm appropriate action, as JCOPE did in the place of the New York General Assembly? Would not that substantially augment your chamber's status in the eyes of the public?

Most legislatures carry out the oversight responsibility with rules of conduct that are part of the operating rules of the chamber. For example, the Pennsylvania House of Representatives created an ethical conduct code and an Ethics Committee to enforce it. It also has rules on the status of members indicted or convicted of a crime. [4] The Pennsylvania House provides a Members Handbook on Ethics and requires all members to take two hours of training each session.

To determine the scope of ethical rules in the House or Senate of any particular state legislature, go to the homepage of the website for that legislature and find the rules for each house. Strong and consistent implementation of these rules is essential to restoring and continuing public confidence. In addition to the rules of each chamber in each legislature, many states have an independent ethics commission that also has oversight over ethical questions of its legislators.

According to the National Conference of State Legislatures, forty-one states have an ethics commission that provides external oversight on legislative and executive branches' ethics. Seven states have more than one ethics oversight body. Alaska, for example, has both an independent ethics commission and a legislative ethics committee. Nine states—Arizona, Idaho, New Hampshire, New Mexico, North Dakota, South Dakota, Vermont, Virginia and Wyoming—do not have an ethics commission. In these states the oversight comes from the legislature itself, or the Department of State or Attorney General. For the details in each state see the website of the National Conference of State Legislatures: www.ncsl.org/research/ethics/state-ethics-commissions.

The NCSL website summarizes the ethics commission in each state and also provides the website for each state ethics commission. The NCSL has dedicated staff assigned to ethics questions that work with all of the legislatures and is a great source of information on ethical questions and regulatory oversight.

Many of the state ethics commissions, as well as the legislative ethics committees, will provide a letter of guidance to legislators who request them. Legislators with doubts about a course of conduct they contemplate should consider consulting the ethics committee or its staff in their chamber and then, depending on the situation, ask for a letter from the committee or external commission.

What more can a legislature do to protect its integrity and maintain public confidence? Most important is that the leadership of both parties in both chambers set an example of ethical behavior and make it clear that they expect members to follow their example and comport themselves within the rules. As one counsel of a legislative ethics committee told me, there must be "top down" leadership. It is the leaders of each chamber who determine the ethical environment of a legislature.

Some state legislatures now require every member and staff to participate in an ethics training course every session. For example, Rule 47 of the Pennsylvania House of Representatives now provides that "Each member shall be required to complete two hours of ethics education and training each legislative session." This can be very helpful, especially if the leadership enthusiastically supports it.

Will this prevent future ethical violations? Probably not, but it should certainly reduce the number of such violations. As indicated earlier, legislators are subject to all of the frailties of other human beings. They are by nature problem solvers and do not like "No" for an answer. Sometimes they get so involved in the "ball game" that they forget the rules. Hopefully, strong legislative leadership and training sessions will encourage recognition of the need to say "No" when an ethical line is about to be crossed.

Legislatures, however, are not seminaries. They cannot teach the basic difference between right and wrong. Individual legislators come to the capitol with whatever moral compass they were raised with at home. A state capitol, with all its pressures and temptations, is not the place to learn a moral code of conduct. Rather, the capitol may be the ultimate testing ground for the strength of that code. On this point all legislators must be accountable to themselves and their constituents.

NOTES

1. Art. II, Sec. 7 of the Pennsylvania Constitution.
2. "List of state and local political scandals in the United States," from the website en.wikipedia.org/wiki/List_of_state_and_local_political_scandals_in_the United_States.
3. The information for the Lopez cases is taken from the reporting of David Hakim and his colleagues at *The New York Times* as reported from August 26, 2012 through November 13, 2013, as well as the report of the New York State Joint Commission on Public Ethics dated February 12, 2013, (JCOPE Report No. 127) found online.
4. Rules of the Pennsylvania House of Representatives. See website:www.legis.state .pa.us.

Chapter Five

The Expenditure of
Money Meant to Influence

Money—which Jesse Unruh called the mother's milk of politics[1] —is spent in several ways to influence state legislators: through direct campaign contributions, through independent campaign expenditures and through lobbying. Expenditures for lobbying and campaigns are constitutionally protected free speech and of themselves are not a problem. The problem is the great amounts of money spent in contributions and lobbying that creates the impression that legislators are unduly influenced or even "bought" by the dispensers of the funding. As pointed out in Chapter Two, twenty-four states revolted against the "republican form" of government by authorizing the initiative and referendum legislative process because of the belief that their legislators were so under the control of affluent interests that they could not be trusted to act in the public interest.

Lobbying and campaign fundraising have points in common. Campaign contributors and those who employ lobbyists expect something in return. They hope the legislatures will implement their views on issues. The expenditures never stop. Legislators are continuously raising funds and lobbyists are relentless in pursuing their principals' interests. The amount of money spent for campaigns and lobbying continues to increase.

In the abstract there is nothing wrong with this. Of course people are going to contribute to candidates who share their views, and others will employ lobbyists to secure specific legislative goals. The question for legislators is how to regulate the money spent to influence them in such a way that their personal integrity and their chamber are not compromised. How can legislators preclude access to their offices by contributors and avoid sliding into the hallmark of corruption, the *quid pro quo*, dollars in exchange for favors?

CAMPAIGN CONTRIBUTIONS

In my first campaign for the Pennsylvania House in 1966, I defeated the senior Republican in the House with a campaign that cost $7500 in a district of 60,000 people. With that money we made two mailings, bought radio time on three stations and newspaper ads in three newspapers, printed brochures for distribution, and ran a small campaign headquarters. There were no computers or electronic communications and television was too expensive. In my 1976 campaign for the State Senate I won with a budget of $75,000 and that, too, was enough to cover a campaign headquarters, radio on five stations, newspapers ads, two mailings and some television.

Such sums are relics of the ancient past. In the 2009–10 session the average raised by a winning candidate for the Pennsylvania House was $119,173, fifteen times what I spent in 1966. For the Senate the average raised by a winning candidate was $323,052—more than four times what I spent in 1976.[2] The averages can, of course, be misleading. The amount needed to win varies by district, depending on its geographical size, the party registration figures and need for election. In some Pennsylvania House seats, the cost has been as high $1 million.[3]

Across the nation the average cost of winning a House seat varies from the low of $773 in New Hampshire to the high of $711,984 in California. For the Senate the average cost to win ranges from $12,523 in Vermont to $843,919 in California.[4] See the "Follow the Money" website for the figures on each state.

How is a constituent or legislator to know or find out the sources of the money given to campaigns and how the candidates spend it? How does a state regulate money in its elections? The National Conference of State Legislatures (NCSL) has devoted considerable attention to these questions and maintains a website that describes the ways campaign money is regulated and contains information on each state. Go to www.ncsl.org/legislatures-elections/elections/campaign-finance-an-overview.aspx.

There are three ways to regulate money in state legislative elections—disclosure of contributions and expenditures, placing limits on the amount anyone can contribute, and public financing of campaigns. The NCSL website provides an overview of contribution limits and states offering public financing for campaigns.

Public disclosure of campaign spending and contributions is the best way to preclude the impression that money will unduly affect the legislature.

> ...The value of disclosure in preventing corruption cannot be understated....[By] revealing information about the contributors to and participants in public discourse and debate, disclosure laws help ensure that voters have the

facts they need to evaluate the various messages competing for their attention.[5]

Since all fifty states require some level of disclosure, the best place to find the law for your state is the home page of the office that runs elections in your state. For example, in Pennsylvania, the Department of State maintains a website devoted to voting and elections with a list of topics that includes the campaign finance law, campaign finance report searches, deadlines for reporting and campaign finance reporting forms.[6]

Although all states have campaign finance disclosure laws, they vary in the detail required, the frequency of reporting, and—perhaps most important—the ease of accessibility for the public. What good is a disclosure law if the public cannot readily see it?

The *Harrisburg Patriot* raised this point in its editorial of April 25, 2012.

> ...Why is the state of Pennsylvania still accepting paper copies of campaign finance reports?...The state is way behind in its posting reports on its website. [In the primary election] there were 372 people running for the House and only 339 reports filed on line when there should have been at least 744 reports (one for March and one for April)...[to give] the public better access to this information: Require all candidates to file their reports online....The public deserves to have timely campaign finance reporting.

Fortunately, the Campaign Disclosure Project has examined and evaluated the disclosure law in each state for the purpose of bringing sunlight to political money. The results are posted in "Grading State Disclosure: 2008" and can be found at www.campaigndisclosure.org/gradingstate/index.html. Using an A through F scale, this site grades the disclosure law for each of the 50 states, provides a database of state disclosure laws, and provides a campaign finance disclosure model law.

According to the report, the states that provided the best access to campaign finance records in 2008 were Washington, Ohio, Oregon, Michigan, Rhode Island and Texas (tied for 4th), California, Florida and Maryland (tied for 7th) and Illinois and Pennsylvania (tied for 10th). The ten states with the weakest access were Connecticut, Vermont, Iowa, Montana, Nevada, Mississippi, Alabama and Delaware (tied for 47th), South Dakota and Wyoming.

The grade and rank for each state is determined by its disclosure law, electronic filing, accessibility, and usability of its records. Pennsylvania, for example, has an overall grade of C-Plus, derived from a B for the law, an F on electronic filing, A for accessibility and a C-Minus for usability.

Although the Campaign Disclosure Project report was written six years ago, it should not be disregarded. There is nothing more recent, but it provides a benchmark for each state against which its progress since 2008 can be measured. I encourage everyone interested in disclosure to review the infor-

mation on this website and then review the disclosure law and accessibility
for their state, comparing the two. Some states have made changes since
2008 but some probably have not. What has happened in your state?

The Citizens United Case and State Campaign Finance Law

In the now famous *Citizens United vs. FEC* case, the Supreme Court of the
United States ruling made a significant change in both federal and state
campaign finance law. The court ruled that as a matter of free speech under
the First Amendment, the federal government may not prohibit or limit independent expenditures by corporations and unions on elections, or independent money spent apart from the candidates and their party committees.[7]
Independent expenditures cannot be coordinated with the campaigns of the
candidate. Contributions to candidates and their committees may be prohibit-
ed, but independent expenditures on elections may not be.

NCSL has reported that in 17 of the 24 states with laws affected by
Citizens United, bills have been offered to amend their laws dealing with
campaign expenditures by corporations and non-profit organizations. The
NCSL website provides a link to the bills introduced.[8] See the NCSL Website for a state-by-state summary of how state laws are affected by the *Citizens United* case.

Some states have issued statements or opinions on the impact of the
Citizens United case on that state's law. In Pennsylvania the Department of
State has posted a statement declaring that Section 1633(a) of the Pennsylvania Election Code cannot be administered constitutionally to prohibit a do-
mestic corporation or unincorporated association from making "independent
expenditures." In every other respect the state law "remains in full force and
effect."[9] Montana is the only state to challenge the applicability of the *Citizens United* opinion to itself. It lost. The Montana Supreme Court had ruled
5–2 with a 29-page majority opinion explaining its decision not to apply the
Citizens United case to Montana's anti-corruption act prohibiting corporate
political contributions.[10] This law was enacted in 1912 as an initiative and
referendum proposal by a public outraged by the blatant corruption of the
state government by the copper-mining companies at the turn of the 19th
century. The U.S. Supreme Court reversed the Montana Supreme Court decision summarily, in a one-paragraph *per curiam* opinion.[11]

In spite of the curt dismissal by the U.S. Supreme Court, the opinions of
the Montana Supreme Court are worth the attention of legislators in all of the
states. Both the majority and two dissenting opinions are informative. In
addition to giving an insightful discussion of the U.S. Supreme Court's decision in the *Citizens United* case, they give a clear historical lesson on why
many states revolted against the republican form of government and authorized legislation by the initiative and referendum process, discussed in Chap-

**Figure 5.1.   The Supreme Court of Montana in 2011. It was the only state su-
preme court to challenge the U.S. Supreme Court decision in *Citizens United v.
FEC.* The Montana court ruled 5-2 in 2011 that the *Citizens United* case did not
apply to Montana's campaign finance law. The U.S. Supreme Court summarily
rejected this. Source: courts.mt.gov/supreme/default.mcpx.**

ter Two. Pages 14–18 of the Montana Supreme Court majority opinion are
included in "Readings for the Legislative Spirit."

The Montana case also points state legislators in the right direction to deal
with the increased corporate and nonprofit money that is likely to come to
state campaigns as a result of the *Citizens United* case. States should enact
laws to require full and prompt disclosure of funds spent. Complete and
timely transparency is the right goal.

The impact of the *Citizens United* case was seen in full force by the
American public in the 2012 Presidential campaigns as the "super PACs" for
each candidate bombarded the airways with advertisements paid for by corporations, unions and affluent individuals in unprecedented amounts. This
will be done again in 2016. Super PACs and independent groups are already
preparing for it. By the time of the 2016 election the Republican and Democratic National Committees will be shadows of their former selves, replaced
by the independent organizations.[12]

States too can expect a rising tide of independent campaign expenditures,
let loose by the *Citizens United* case, to surge through their campaigns.
Between 2005 and 2010 independent expenditures totaled 19 percent of the

contributions to candidates and in three of those states the independent expenditure exceeded 25 percent. The amounts will, I believe, grow dramatical-
ly. The Colombia Law School Public Laws and Legal Theory Working Paper
Group studied independent expenditures in depth and concluded

> Our laws are reasonably effective at obtaining and publicizing the identities of
> those who contribute directly to candidates; it is now critical that those laws be
> updated to make them effective at disclosing those donors to independent
> committees. [13]

What is your state doing?

LOBBYING: APPLE PIE AND THE FIRST AMENDMENT

Lobbying[14] —seeking to influence what the government is doing—is as
American as apple pie. The First Amendment to the U.S. Constitution is clear
on the point: "Congress shall make no law ... abridging the freedom of
speech or ... of the right of the people peacefully to assemble, and to petition
the government for a redress of grievances."

Yet the misuse or distortion of this right by some of those paid to advocate to the government has tarnished lobbying to the point that the public is at
best skeptical of it and in many cases profoundly distrustful of it.[15] As
discussed in Chapter One, based on the perception that their legislatures were
controlled by lobbyists, twenty-four states took the exclusive power to legislate out of the hands of the legislatures under the initiative and referendum
process. And now every state has laws requiring the registration of those
involved in lobbying and requiring a public report of the amounts spent
doing it.

Of course these laws apply only to those who are paid to advocate to the
government. An individual writing or talking to his state legislator is exempt
from these laws. The world of lobbying is therefore divided into two
camps—citizens acting on their own or in collaboration with others without
remuneration, and professionals who are paid to advocate for their clients.
The professional camp is now so large, well organized and influential that
Alan Rosenthal, eminent scholar of state legislatures, wrote a book on it
titled *The Third House* (of the state legislatures).[16]

Lobbying on a professional basis is as honorable a profession as law,
medicine, accounting, or public relations. But as in the other professions,
wayward lobbyists have given a black eye to their colleagues. The most
egregious example is at the federal level, where Jack Abramoff of K Street
infamy went to prison for several years and is now advocating that former
and executive members of Congress should be precluded from lobbying.

Professional lobbying is expensive, but lobbying expenses are tax deductions for businesses and there is no limit on the amount that can be spent. In 2011 the amount spent on lobbying the Texas legislature was almost $300 million.[17]

Virtually every industry or organization regulated by a state government has on its staff or employs lobbyists to advocate on its behalf and protect its interests. Bankers, electric and gas utilities, organized labor, non-profit companies, highway contractors, insurance companies and natural gas drillers quickly come to mind. Their lobbyists are unrelenting on behalf of their principals, as they should be. There is nothing wrong with this, as long as those involved in lobbying comply with the law. Based on my experience, the vast majority do.

Considering the huge amount of money spent on lobbying and its potential impact on the legislative process it is surprising to learn, as I did, that there is no single website or source readily available to the public that shows the amounts spent on lobbying in each state. The Follow the Money project in Helena, Montana, is beginning to assemble such a site and currently has posted the information on five states—California, Louisiana, Maryland, Texas, and Wisconsin.[18] For each of these states the site shows the total client expenditures, total lobbying firm expenditures, total lobbyist expenditures and the Grand Total of all lobbying expenditures. Follow the Money can only provide information on five states so far because of the time and work needed to collect the data.

Follow the Money is working with Open Government and will be posting information on other states as circumstances permit.[19] The difficulty in obtaining the information on the other 45 states is not necessarily caused by the state or the lobbyists practicing there. Some states have voluntarily made such information readily available to the public. For example, the State of Washington Public Disclosure Commission website provides links that show Lobbyist Expenditure Summary Reports that include the following for lobbyists: total compensation, personal expenses, entertainment, contributions, advertising, political advertising, and other expenses. For lobbyist employers the site reports total compensation, expenditures, and contributions.[20]

The Washington site has a chart showing the total amount spent on lobbying from 2001 to the present. For 2011 the total was $53,443,256 and for 2012 through July 15 the total was $25,630,759. The same site shows the amount spent by each employer and their lobbyists, including the name and salaries of the lobbyists.

States vary widely in their definitions of regulated lobbying and the reporting/disclosure requirements. To evaluate your state go to the NCSL website and look at "How States Define," "Lobbying" and "Lobbyist," and "Links to States' Legislative Ethics and Lobbying Laws." Each of these provides the link to each state's website.[21]

The state laws requiring registration of lobbying principals and the reporting of the expenses paid by them have not clearly settled the line between compensated lobbying and the distribution of educational information. The American Legislative Exchange Council (ALEC) is a case in point. A Sec. 501(c) (3) non-profit entity under the Internal Revenue Code, ALEC is financed by corporations that spend millions each year to host corporate lobbyists and state legislators at national conferences to discuss issues, issue bulletins to legislators recommending votes on pending bills, and draft model press releases for legislators to use in pushing the ALEC model bills. All of this is done without ALEC registering or reporting as a lobbyist, in spite of the fact that legislators may receive scholarships from ALEC's corporate donors or can attend ALEC conferences at the taxpayers' expenses.

As reported by Paul Abowd in *Mother Jones* of May 8, 2012, the ALEC failure to register under state lobbying laws is now under attack from Common Cause.[22] In some states—South Carolina, Colorado and Indiana—ALEC is specifically exempted by name from registering and reporting under the lobbying laws.

The controversy created by the relatively recent realization of ALEC's exemption from lobbying registration and reporting has motivated fourteen of ALEC's corporate members, including Coca-Cola, McDonald's and Proctor & Gamble, to drop out of the group.

ALEC, of course, takes a different view, arguing that it is a proper non-profit educational entity. See the ALEC website: www.alec.org. This website provides a full report on the creation of this organization in 1973 by a group of legislators and conservative policy advocates in Chicago; it has since grown to the point that it operates a number of task forces that have developed several hundred model bills on state issues. According to the website, each year close to 1,000 bills, based at least in part on ALEC model Legislation, are introduced in the states. Of these, an average of 20 percent becomes law.

The website carries the ALEC Formula for Success that concludes,

> Since its founding, ALEC has amassed an unmatched record of achieving groundbreaking changes in public policy. Policies such as teacher competency testing, pension reform, and enterprise zones represent just a handful of ALEC's victories in the states.[23]

Because each state has its own definition of lobbying that requires registration and reporting, the ALEC case will probably be decided on a state-by-state basis. The case presents a fundamental question of how far national, out-of state-organizations can go to propose or pursue legislative goals in an individual state without registering and reporting under state law. When does "education" become "advocacy"?

The ability to pay great costs involved in hiring lobbyists, providing their staff, and paying for entertainment and hospitality and public relations through television provides a huge advantage over those who do not have the funding to compete. Corporations, non-profit trade associations and unions lobby on an entirely different level than those who may question those groups' positions but lack the funding to employ professional lobbyists.

A good example occurred in Pennsylvania when the natural gas industry hired a popular former governor, Tom Ridge, and his firm for $1 million to be its chief public voice for a year.[24] There is nothing improper or wrong with this. Ridge registered as a lobbyist and complied with the laws.

The uneven playing field of lobbying created by the funding required to pursue it presents a challenge for legislators. The challenge is how to maintain a proper "arm's length" relationship with lobbyists without compromising their independence of judgment. For a legislator to value information received from a lobbyist does not mean that the legislator is compromised. There is no reason legislators cannot appreciate lobbyists without being "in their pockets." Lobbyists can be very helpful to legislators, particularly in providing accurate information on their clients so the legislators can better judge the impact of the legislation before them.

There are steps the public can seek to bring about the proper relationship between legislators and lobbyists. The most effective by far is a statute that requires full and complete disclosure of lobbying efforts be readily available to the public. The State of Washington Public Disclosure Commission discussed earlier is a good example. The Follow the Money and Open Government projects will be breaking new ground in opening this thicket. You can also look at the State of Minnesota Lobbying Disclosure Law, widely acknowledged for its salutary effect with full and timely disclosure. Go to the website of the Minnesota Campaign Finance and Public Disclosure Board and review the Lobbyist Handbook it has published.

Review the lobbying disclosure law for your state that can be found through the NCSL website. Then ask the following questions suggested by the NCSL:[25]

Does your state require lobbyists to register and identify their employer?

Does your state require a report from lobbyists on who is being lobbied, how often, and on what topics?

Does your law require reporting of income and connections to public officials?

To what extent does your state prohibit or limit gifts to public officials?

Does your state require reporting the costs of lobbying, including organizing the "grassroots"?

Does your law require the reporting data to be readily available to the public?

Does your law prohibit compensation to lobbyists that is contingent upon the result?

Does your law prohibit false statements in lobbying practices?

Does your law establish a time period before legislators may become lobbyists?

Does your law include in the definition of lobbying "goodwill," such as someone who builds relationships with legislators?

Besides seeking to improve your own state law, there is one other major initiative you can take—organize your own lobbying effort that is built around volunteers and use of the Internet. This will be discussed in the last chapter.

NOTES

1. Bill Boyarsky, *Big Daddy: Jesse Unruh and the Art of Power Politics* (Los Angeles: University of California, 2008),

2. Follow the Money website: www.followthemoney.org/Institut/index.phtm.

3. The special election in June 2000 for the 114th House District in Lackawanna County, PA, which determined control of the House.

4. Follow The Money of the National Institute on Money in State Politics (online). Nationwide the total spent on state House campaigns in 2007–8 was $608,400, 563 and for the Senate campaigns $357,345,096, a combined total of $965,745,000.

5. Montana Supreme Court Justice Beth Baker dissenting in the Montana case, 2011 MT 238 at page 34.

6. Pennsylvania Department of State website: www.dos.state.us/bcel.

7. 130 S. Ct. 876, 171 L. Ed. 2010 (2010).

8. NCSL website, Life After *Citizens United* and States Respond to *Citizens United*.

9. Pennsylvania Department of State website.

10. *Western Traditions Partnerships v. Bullock,* 2011 MT 328(2011).

11. *American Traditions Partnerships v. Bullock,* 567 U.S. (2012). The people of Montana have not acquiesced in the Supreme Court's decision in this case. In 2012 Initiative 166 was drafted to direct the state's Congressional delegation to propose an amendment to the U.S. Constitution that would invalidate *Citizens United* by declaring that corporations are not human and not entitled to the same constitutional rights as human beings. This initiative received overwhelming approval at the November 6, 2012 election: 314,000 to 100,000. See Montana Corporate Contributions Initiative 1–166(2012). Ballotpedia website.

12. Marcus Gold, "Super PACs and Other Interest Groups Already Setting Pace for the 2016 Presidential Race," *POLITICO* (July 23, 2013).

13. Richard Briffault, Paper Number 12–297, "Updating Disclosure for the New Era of Independent Spending," Columbia Law School, Public Law & Legal Theory Working Paper Group, April 16, 2012.

14. The author has been a registered lobbyist in Pennsylvania for fifteen years and now lobbies with Malady & Wooten, a Harrisburg government affairs firm. He was the course planner and chair of the PA Bar Association's Continuing Legal Education program on complying with the state's Lobbying Disclosure Law.

15. A poll by the Princeton Survey Research Associates International for the Public Affairs Council showed that 55 percent of Americans view companies that hire lobbyists unfavorably with only seven percent viewing them more favorably and 34 percent having no opinion. However, when presented with a range of reasons for a company to engage directly with the government, the public by and large approves of lobbying activities. Andrew Joseph, "Influence Alley," *National Journal* (Nov 15, 2011).

16. Alan Rosenthal, *The Third House: Lobbyists and Lobbying in the States* (Washington, DC: CQ Press), 2001.

17. Follow the Money website, Lobbying Expenditures Overview.

18. Ibid.

19. OpenGovernment.org/ Current Status.

20. State of Washington Public Disclosure Commission Lobbyist Expenditure Report: www.pdc.wa.gov.

21. NCSL website, www.ncsl.org: "How States Define "Lobbying" and Lobbyist" and "Links to States' Legislative Ethics and Lobbying Laws.

22. Paul Abowd, "ALEC Gets a Break from State Lobbying Laws," Mother Jones (May 8, 2012).

23. ALEC website. www.ALEC.org.

24. Aura Olson, "Ridge's Shale Coalition Contract Expires," *Pittsburgh Post-Gazette* (August 5, 2011).

25. Peggy Kerns, "The Influence Business," *State Legislatures Magazine* (January 2009).

Chapter Six

Reapportionment of State Legislative and U.S. Congressional Districts

One of the heaviest questions for any state is how to prepare a plan for the boundaries of the state House and Senate seats, as well as the U.S. Congressional districts, after each federal census so that they have the same number of people and meet other standards. In Pennsylvania, for example, the constitution requires that municipalities may not be divided unless absolutely necessary.[1]

Meeting this responsibility goes to the heart of legislative integrity. To the extent a legislative district plan does not meet the one-person, one-vote standard for population equality and any other requirements, the state legislature is an invalidly constituted body. It cannot enact legislation unless it is truly representative of the population.

Except to legislative "insiders," legislative redistricting is usually (but not always, as will be discussed in Chapter 8) an obscure subject of which most people are unaware and in which they have no interest. In "Does Representation Matter to Me?"[2] Amanda Holt, a Harrisburg "outsider" who became quite involved in the Pennsylvania redistricting process, put it this way:

> Why care about representation? It seems like an obscure issue, far removed from the everyday life of citizens. The reality is that representation stands at the core of our liberty, closely intertwined into our daily activities....Many other issues addressed at a state level touch close to home, like education, roads, and safety. When Pennsylvanians gather to discuss these state issues, who will speak on your behalf?

Before 1962, the redistricting of state legislative seats was not an issue in which courts were involved. It was thought to be political, a matter for each state legislature to handle. That was changed forever when the Mayor of Nashville, Tennessee, brought a case in the federal courts alleging that the people of Nashville were denied the equal protection of the law given by the 14th Amendment to the U.S. Constitution.[3]

Tennessee legislative seats were apportioned by county, without regard to population. Nashville had grown significantly but its numerical representation at the state capitol remained the same. The case reached the Supreme Court of the United States, which decided in favor of the Mayor, ruling that federal courts have the jurisdiction to judge the constitutionality of legislative re-districting under the equal protection clause of the 14th Amendment.[4]

A year later the U.S. Supreme Court in *Gray vs. Sanders* provided a concept that in later cases became the federal constitutional standard for judging state legislative districting plans—one-person, one-vote.[5] As implemented, this standard meant that all seats in a legislative districting plan must have the same population to the extent practical.

Meeting the federal standards in redistricting is a time-consuming, intricate task. Each state must first take the population figures from the Federal Census Bureau and relate them to the municipal boundary lines used by the state.[6] A new plan is then drawn for the House and Senate seats providing for equal population representation in each seat. Drawing seats in rural areas of relatively stable populations can be relatively simple, but in urban and suburban areas of changing populations it is particularly intricate work. How, for example, do you draw House seats in suburban Philadelphia, Pennsylvania, without dividing municipalities, and produce districts of equal populations?

Computers have greatly facilitated redistricting according to population because they can analyze, calculate and allocate numbers with electronic speed. Computers can produce the information needed by those doing the redistricting plan, but only the humans doing it can make the necessary judgments, such as when it is appropriate to divide municipalities.

In the words of Shakespeare, this is where "the rub" is. Human nature being what it is, those in the majority party of a legislature will want to do the redistricting to protect their incumbent members and their control. Notwithstanding that inclination of legislators, most states leave the redistricting in the hands of the legislature itself.

In Georgia, for example, the House and Senate each have standing committees for the re-apportionment of that chamber. According to its website, the Georgia legislative committees have held twelve joint public hearings across the state to get public input into the legislative redistricting process.[7] The redistricting plan developed by these standing legislative committees is introduced and passed like any other legislation.

The perception that the redistricting process has been abused to protect the incumbents has caused thirteen states to take redistricting out of the hands of the legislatures altogether and give it to a commission.

Pennsylvania's redistricting is done by a commission of four legislators and a fifth non-member[8] chosen by the other four, or, if they cannot agree, by the State Supreme Court. The legislature itself does not approve the plan. The plan becomes law without going through the legislative process if the Commission approves it and it is not appealed to and rejected in the Supreme Court.

New Jersey has given redistricting to a commission of eleven non-legislators. The New Jersey Apportionment Commission consists of ten members appointed in equal numbers by the state chairs of the Democratic and Republican Parties and an eleventh member is appointed by the Commission or, if the Commission cannot agree, the chief justice of the state Supreme Court. The New Jersey Commission maintains a website that declares the Commission "is eager to engage the residents of the state and provides information on public meeting schedules, information and dates and how to sign up or contact it. See the Commission website: www.apportionmentcomission.org.

California has tried to remove redistricting as far as possible from partisan political influence. The California Citizens Redistricting Commission was created by the voters as Proposition 11 of the November 2008 election. The Commission has fourteen members—five Democrats, five Republicans and four Declined-to-State—chosen in a unique manner. Persons interested in serving on the Commission submit their applications online. Those who are qualified are invited to submit a supplemental application in which they answer questions in essay form. Independent auditors from the State Audit Bureau select 120 from these applications—40 Republicans, 40 Democrats, and 40 Declined-to-State. Following interviews, the 120 are reduced to 60 and the names sent to the leaders of both parties in both Houses. The leaders, like lawyers in picking a jury, have the peremptory right to remove 24 from the pool. The Audit Bureau then draws randomly from the pool three Democrats, three Republicans, and two Declined-to-State. A month later the eight selected chose six more from the pool, two from each party and two from Declined-to-State. The selections are valid for ten years, but the work is done in the first year.[9]

The California Commission posts all information on its website and places great emphasis on citizens' involvement.

> The Commission is relying on the active participation of citizens across California to weigh in on how the districts should be drawn....This is an open conversation that will assist the Commission in evaluating citizen input and exercising responsible judgment about what districts should look like—a computer can never do that.

The National Conference of State Legislatures has done considerable work to make redistricting plan formation available online to the public.[10]

The NCSL website gives links to the redistricting website in each of the 50 states. Google "NCSL State Redistricting Websites" or go to: www.ncsl.org/legislatures-elections/redist/links-to-state-legislative-redistricting-web.

Another NCSL website displays the 2010 NCSL Congressional and State Legislative Redistricting Deviation Table that shows the ideal size for each seat and the per cent of deviation from that ideal. Go to: www.ncsl.org/legislatures-elections/redist/links-to-state-legislative-redistricting-deviation-table.aspx.

There is no perfect redistricting system, one assured of producing a fairly balanced plan that conforms to the federal one-man, one-vote rule and the state requirements. But there are ways to judge how closely your state's redistricting system comes to the ideal. Using the information provided above and from the appropriate websites, ask these questions:

Is your system transparent?

Is the important information publicly available online in a timely fashion?

Is the public invited to participate and does it have the opportunity to do so in a timely manner?

Does the public have the opportunity to review and comment on the final plan after it is proposed and before it is adopted?

Does the proposed plan meet the requirements of your state constitution and the federal one-person, one-vote rule?

Does the proposed plan create districts that are so lopsided in party registration that they are not competitive in a general election?

NOTES

1. Art. II, Sec. 17 of the PA Constitution.
2. Blog site. AmandaE/com.
3. Amendment 14. Citizenship Rights. Sec. 1. "All persons born or naturalized in the United States, and subject to the jurisdiction thereof, are citizens of the United States and of the state wherein they reside. No state shall make or enforce any law which shall abridge the privileges or immunities of citizens of the United States; nor shall any state deprive any person of life, liberty, or property, without due process of law; nor deny to any person within its jurisdiction the equal protection of the laws."
4. *Baker v. Carr*, 369 U.S. 186 (1962).
5. *Gray v. Sanders*, 372 U.S. 368 (1963).
6. The boundary lines used by the U.S. Census Bureau and the states do not always correlate and therefore some states must "clean up" the federal lines so they are can use them. Conversation with Mark McKillop, Legislative Services Director for the Senate of PA. Democratic Staff, July 31, 2012.
7. Georgia website.
8. Art. II, Sec. 18 of the PA Constitution.
9. Wedrawthelines.ca.gov.
10. At the "NCSL Legislative Redistricting" you will find a treasure trove of sources of information on redistricting—a series of redistricting and election forum presentations, a 2010

redistricting law publication, a state legislative redistricting website, a table of 21 states with redistricting commissions, materials from previous redistricting seminars, and the presentations from a national redistricting seminar held in Washington, DC, in 2011.

III

The Ultimate Question—
Why Are You Here
at Your State Capital?

Chapter Seven

Legislators

The work of state legislatures has never been more difficult or more challenging. Consider, for example, the unfunded pension liability that Lou Cannon, a veteran reporter on state government, has described as "a runaway freight train bearing down on state and local governments."[1] A State Budget Commission Task Force led by former New York Lt. Governor Richard Ravitch and Federal Reserve Chairman Paul Volcker studied the unfunded pension liability question in California, Illinois, New Jersey, New York, Texas and Virginia. They concluded that the unfunded state government pension obligation could be as high as $3 trillion, in addition to another $1 trillion in unfunded healthcare cost obligation.[2] This is three times more than the $1.53 trillion appropriated to operate all of the 50 states in 2010. Without funding for these obligations, state governments will be required to make major reductions in important programs, such as education, police protection, transportation, and social services.[3]

There is more. As Lou Cannon points out in the NCSL's *State Legislatures Magazine,* there are issues comparable in terms of social impact and incendiary nature which confront the states, including paying for rising health care costs, education, immigration, collective bargaining and same-sex marriage. Regardless of what the Congress in Washington does, states will need to deal with these issues. And the longer it takes the Congress to resume governing in a functional manner, the more important it is for state legislatures to act effectively. Resolving these issues will be a difficult assignment and require all of the legislative talent that state legislatures can summon.

In the face of incendiary, complicated issues like these, why do you want to come to the capitol as a Representative or Senator?

There is probably no single answer for any single legislator. Most people have multiple motivations. The answer might include the following, in some combination and in varying degrees of importance: a desire to help solve the political issues like those just listed, or a desire to carry out your political party's policies, or to reduce government as much as possible, to help people, or to make it a career because you are qualified for the work and the pay and retirement benefits are attractive.

Whatever your answer, the most important thing an aspiring legislator can do is disclose the answer to his constituents so that there is no gap between what the legislator says he or she will do and what he or she actually does. Sailing under false colors is dangerous and can produce heavy political damage.

Assuming a successful election, how do you relate to your colleagues in the House or Senate chamber? There are a number of subsidiary questions that deserve the legislator's contemplation.

Figure 7.1.   Tennessee Supreme Court Chief Justice Gary R. Wade swears into office State Representative Raumesh Akbari in Nashville, January 14, 2014. Akbari replaced Lois DeBerry, who died in 2013. Source: Mark Humphrey/AP/CORBIS.

Do you have any sense of idealism about the legislature as an institution? Does the fact that Thomas Jefferson and his 56 colleagues put their lives on the line signing the Declaration of Independence to defend free legislatures ignite any sparks of idealism in your sense of the legislature?

Do you view the House or Senate as an institution that is larger than either political party or both parties combined? During my tenure in the Pennsylvania Senate there was a President Pro Tempore, Martin Murray, who believed very strongly in this. Every Monday night in session he held an open hospitality suite in his office for Senators of both parties where they could relax, review the day, and speak their minds. Although he was a strong Democrat, Murray himself was available to counsel or talk with any Senator. The occasion was known as "Marty's Bar and Grill" or "Father Murray's Confessional," but those monikers mislead on the salutary effect that they had on the Senate of Pennsylvania in helping it stay on keel as an institution. Senator Murray went to some lengths to facilitate Democratic and Republican Senators talking to each other—and they did.

Are you willing to develop diplomatic relations with members of the other party, regardless of how strongly their views differ from yours? The failure to do this is a major complaint about why state legislatures—and certainly the U.S. Congress—are not more productive. Alan Rosenthal has called state legislatures "laboratories of conflict." What will you do to make your "laboratory" one in which conflict is resolved in the best tradition of James Madison and the other Constitution writers?

One of the experiences I most value from my service in the Senate was developing such a relationship with two of the most conservative Republicans so that we could agree on a major reform of the system by which the Senate confirms the Governor's nominations in Pennsylvania. The Senate Democratic leadership might have passed something on their own but they knew that if the reform was to have a lasting effect, it needed to be done on a bipartisan basis. Richard Frame and Stanley Stroup, the Republican leaders, and I, as Chair of the Committee, agreed that we would discuss the problem over private dinners. We held four or five such dinners, limited to the five members of the committee and our staff. The press was excluded intentionally. In fact, the existence of the dinners was kept secret from everyone but the Senate leadership. When we finished our work, the Republicans and I were not close to being personal friends, but we did have respect for each other. Our recommendations became law. That would not have occurred without our private dinners.[4]

What are you doing to do to make your work and the work of your chamber transparent to your constituents? Will you take advantage of the social media tools now in common use—Twitter, Blog, Facebook, YouTube—to let your constituents know what you are doing, including how you are spending their money?

Are you as willing as Pennsylvania's State Representatives Eugene De-Pasquale and Lynda Schlegel Culver are to post your expenses on your website? DePasquale, now the state's Auditor General, showed how much he received for capitol per diems, committee meeting per diems, an auto lease, constituent service office purchases (e.g., office lease, parking, supplies, publications, flags and postage) and miscellaneous. Under "monthly legislative expenses," Schlegel Culver shows her district office rent, trash service, flags, office supplies, cooler and water supplies, and clerical services.[5]

The social media tools have opened a vast, although not fully understood, opportunity to communicate with the constituencies and public at large. The NCSL has put considerable effort into understanding the use of the social media by legislatures. NCSL maintains a Legislative Social Media Site that shows social media being used in each state. In addition, NCSL has a companion website "Policies Related to Legislative Use of Social Media" that provides the legislative policies of the states that have them.[6] As NCSL points out, the use of social media by legislatures presents a bit of a thicket on questions like privacy, conflicts with statutes, use of advertisements, and open records laws. Nevertheless, the use of social media can greatly help legislators in communicating with constituents.

Social media have expanded the manner in which legislators can communicate on issues. In June 2013 State Senator Wendy Davis of Texas received statewide and national attention for her filibuster against a bill to further restrict abortions in Texas. *The New York Times* carried a headline, "From Statehouse to YouTube, a Filibuster is a Hit." Her speech was shown through the Senate's website but that looked comically old-fashioned compared to what viewers saw on YouTube. It was through YouTube that Senator Davis' filibuster was widely seen and shared.[7]

The most embarrassing moments for legislators come when the public learns something that takes it by surprise. The midnight pay raise discussed in Chapter Three is a good example. To avoid that kind of disaster, legislatures should lay appropriate groundwork for what they want to accomplish by hearings, floor discussion and public disclosure in advance.

It has been suggested that everything a legislature does must be done in the "sunshine" of public openness. This can be a serious impediment to legislative productiveness.

There are two processes that ought to take place behind closed doors, so to speak. The first is legislative caucuses, where the parties discuss the legislation they will be acting on. The other is negotiation to resolve serious differences. Several years ago the Pennsylvania legislature put its budget conference committees effectively under the "sunshine" law. All discussions between the House and Senate on budget settlements had to be done in public. This was a serious mistake. Nothing happened at these public meetings. Negotiations cannot take place in public. My committee on Senate

Confirmation Reform would have failed if we had held our meetings in public. There is one addendum. While budget negotiations and comparable issue resolutions are best done in private, the parties must make full disclosure on their agreement when they have reached it. Consider the U.S. Constitutional Convention of 1787. The entire four months of meeting was done behind guarded closed doors, with the public and the press excluded.[8] Of course, the Federalist Papers were widely distributed and explained what the constitution writers had worked out.

Are you willing to use the assistance that legislative staff can provide? This may sound like a naïve question, but Karl Kurtz and Tim Rice, experts on legislative staffing from their own work in legislatures and the NCSL, are concerned that an influx of new legislators do not value staff services.[9] In my experience, staffing is essential to effectiveness.[10] The staff can be enormously valuable in evaluating requests by lobbyists. They can produce ideas and guidance that help keep the legislator on track.

The late Governor of Pennsylvania, Robert P. Casey, had a question for everyone who has held public office: "What did you do with the power of your office when you had it?" That is a question every legislator should ponder while in office. When your legislative service is over, how will you answer that question? There will be a multitude of problems, challenges and

Figure 7.2.   Protestors occupy the Wisconsin capitol at Madison on February 25, 2011. Source: Darren Halick/Reuters/CORBIS.

temptations that you and your colleagues will face between taking the oath of office and your departure. I hope this book has furnished helpful guidance as you navigate the minefields of legislative service. The ultimate job is yours. As President Kennedy often said, the only sure reward for public service is a satisfied conscience.

NOTES

1. Lou Cannon, "The Conservative Difference," *State Legislatures Magazine* (July/August 2012), 17.

2. John Celock, "Paul Volcker, Richard Ravitch Say State Budget Threatens 'Social Order,'" *The Huffington Post* (July 17, 2012).

3. As of August 18, 2012, the Illinois legislature failed to reach agreement on a pension reform package. At more than $83 billion in unfunded pension liability, Illinois has the largest unfunded obligation in the U.S. See Steve Yaccino, "Illinois Legislature Fails To Agree on Pension Package," *The New York Times* (August 18, 2012), A10.

4. Franklin L. Kury, *Clean Politics, Clean Streams*. (Bethlehem, PA: Lehigh University Press, 2011), 96–97.

5. PA House of Representatives website.

6. NSCL website.

7. Bruce Stetler, "From Statehouse to YouTube A Filibuster is a Hit." *The New York Times* (July 1, 2013), B1.

8. "There was criticism of the secrecy rule; Jefferson did not like it when he heard of it. Yet it is difficult to see how a Constitution could have evolved had the Convention been open to abuse and suggestion from the public. Sentries were placed at the State House doors; members could not copy the daily journal without permission. Secrecy in legislative assemblies was no new thing. All the Revolutionary colonial assemblies were secret; the first Continental Congress had been so of necessity, and Congressional debates still were not reported." Katherine Drinker Bowen, *Miracle at Philadelphia: The Story of the Constitutional Convention, May to September 1787* (Boston: Little, Brown and Co., 1966), 22–23.

9. Karl Kurtz and Tim Rice, "Facing the Future," *State Legislatures Magazine* (July/August 2012), 38–40.

10. Franklin L. Kury, *Clean Politics, Clean Streams: A Legislative Autobiography* (Bethlehem, PA: Lehigh University Press, 2011), 159–60.

Chapter Eight

Constituents

Constituents come to the capitol for the same reason the professional or business lobbyists come—they want to petition the government for a redress of grievances. The constituents want their voices heard. If state legislatures are, as Alan Rosenthal has suggested, laboratories of conflict, they are also the forums for the constituents to test ways to change the status quo or preserve it.

Pennsylvania has recently been the forum for two completely different approaches to seeking change that provide instructive lessons for the other 49 states. One method is the Occupy Harrisburg initiative that sought to do in Pennsylvania what the Occupy Wall Street movement attempted nationally. A stark contrast is the initiative taken by Amanda Holt, a previously unknown music teacher from Allentown, Pennsylvania, whose efforts upset the work of the state Legislative Redistricting Commission and forced it to revise its redistricting plan. The methods used and the results attained are strikingly different.

OCCUPY HARRISBURG'S SIEGE OF THE STATE CAPITOL

The Occupy Harrisburg movement planted its tent on the steps of the Pennsylvania capitol in September 2011, a few weeks after the Occupy Wall Street movement began in New York, and maintained it for fourteen months, closing its effort election week 2012. Occupy Harrisburg adopted the Occupy Wall Street goals of protesting the inequality of 99 percent of Americans against the one percent of wealthy interests until such time as it developed its own goals.

The Occupy Harrisburg group showed persistence in maintaining its location. Like the U.S. Postal Service, neither rain nor snow nor sleet kept them

**Figure 8.1.   Pro-choice rally at the Missouri capitol in Jefferson City. 1989.
Source: Joseph Sohn/Visions of America/CORBIS.**

from holding forth in their redoubt. They were determined to be there for a
long run and took a number of steps to do that. They developed Facebook
and Twitter sites, sponsored rallies, showed motion pictures and distributed
literature.[1]

    High-minded and idealistic as the Occupy Harrisburg members were,
however, they have nothing tangible to show for the effort they expended. If
they have had an impact on legislation or legislators inside the capitol it is
undetected. Occupy Harrisburg, like the other Occupy efforts across the
country, had a more abstract goal and they may have achieved it. As Charles
Blow, writing in *The New York Times*, observed,

    In the end the Occupy movement may have a clear legacy:

> …ingraining in the national conscience the idea that our extreme levels of
> inequality are politically untenable and morally unacceptable and that eventu-
> ally the 99 percent will demand better.[2]

AMANDA HOLT'S LIGHTNING BOLT

The redrawing of Pennsylvania's House and Senate district boundary lines
after each federal census has long been considered an insider's game con-

fined to the leaders of the four legislative caucuses and a fifth, a chairman appointed by them or, if they cannot agree, the state Supreme Court. Under the state constitution, this Legislative Redistricting Commission ("the Commission") prepares a plan based on the new census numbers and holds a hearing on it. The plan takes effect if no one appeals it to the state Supreme Court and that court orders a new plan to be drafted. The legislature itself has no vote on the matter. There is no more "nit-picking," intricate work for a legislature to do than redraw the district lines for 203 House and 50 Senate seats. It is time consuming and tedious. Most of the challenges have been to individual districts, not the state as a whole. The Commission's plans had never been rejected by the Supreme Court and the 2011 Commission plan was expected to be no different. The Commission was composed of the leaders of each party in each house, and the Chair was a retired Superior Court justice appointed by the Supreme Court.

On February 3, 2012, the long-standing impression that the Commission was unchallengeable from the outside was shattered by the decision of the Supreme Court that, for the first time, rejected the Commission's plan and ordered a new one to be drafted.[3] The largest surprise was the basis on which the court acted—the Court based its decision in large measure on information

Figure 8.2.   Amanda Holt, whose persistence precipitated a state Supreme Court ruling that invalidated a proposed legislative apportionment plan. Source: Mindy Holt.

and an alternative plan submitted to it by Amanda Holt, a music teacher from Allentown, a woman with no previous political involvement except that she was a Republican precinct committee person.

Holt and the Senate Democrats were among the appellants from the Commission plan. As the Court notes, "These appellants do not claim that the LRC was obligated to accept their plan, they just offer those plans as proof that the LRC's final Plan contained subdivision splits that were not absolutely necessary."[4]

> A concrete showing has been made that political subdivisions were split, even where the population was smaller than the individual legislative districts and subdivisions were avoidable, and that the number of fractures across the Commonwealth was considerably higher in the Final Plan than *the Holt plan proved was easily achievable. This powerful evidence, challenging the Final Plan as a whole, suffices to show that the Final Plan is contrary to law.* While the LRC was not, and is not, obligated to adopt any of the alternative plans presented to it, it must devise a new plan upon remand.[5] (Emphasis added.)

The Supreme Court's remanding of the plan to the Commission with an order to do another one struck the Commission and the legislature with the force of a powerful lightning bolt. It forced the Commission and legislators seeking re-election to focus on a new plan. How did it happen that a complete outsider could break up the LRCs plans?

According to Holt herself, it started when she and some friends were discussing candidates for office in 2010 and noticed that, although they lived near each other, they had different representatives in the House and Senate. Her curiosity piqued, Holt began to look into the matter, starting with the state constitution. She found Article 11, Section 16, which provides,

> Unless absolutely necessary no county city, incorporated town, borough, township or ward shall be divided in forming either a senatorial or representative district.

The more Amanda Holt reviewed the redistricting process unfolding after the 2011 census the more she became determined to become involved. She spent weeks—over 1,000 hours—reviewing the 2001 map and eventually drawing her own statewide plan. Her plan broke seven fewer counties, 81 fewer municipalities and 184 fewer wards than the Commission House districting map. For the Senate her map also had seven fewer county breaks, two fewer municipal breaks and 22 fewer ward breaks.[6]

Holt put up a blog site, AmandaE.com, and she did it with gusto. The title is "Sharing Insights and Adventures Related to Redistricting, Books, Do-It-Yourself Projects, Politics, Technology and More! *Join The Fun*!"

Among the topics on her blog are:

House Redistricting Recap
Senate Redistricting Recap
Redistricting Testimony Update
Holt Legislative Redistricting 3rd Testimony
Stay Engaged
The Story of Reapportionment
Does Representation Matter to Me?
Watching Harrisburg Legislators

In addition, her blog has links to various proposed district maps.

Holt testified before the Commission and when that Commission rejected her plan, she became one of the appellants that challenged the Commission plan in the Supreme Court of Pennsylvania. The result shook the political world of Harrisburg as few Supreme Court decisions have. Amanda Holt's lightning bolt hit its target.

Holt reminded the legislature of Pennsylvania—and the other 49 states as well—that its work is public work and that every citizen has the right to become fully involved. No legislator in any state can assume that any aspect of legislative work is so intricate or complex that they alone can have the answer to deal with it.

Holt's lightning bolt is also a wake-up call to constituents in every state who are cynical or skeptical that they can have any impact on what their elected legislators are doing. Constituents have undreamed-of power to challenge the status quo, but it takes lots of homework, starting with the state constitution, sustained research, the willingness to reach out and find kindred spirits, the willingness to use blog sites and other social media, and then the discipline to work within the system by talking with legislators and testifying.

Constituents have never had more going for them. No citizenry has ever had more information about its governments available to it than now. Every state has a website showing its constitution, the makeup of the executive and legislative branches, a list of contact information on members, bills pending, committee assignments, and ways for legislators and the governor to be contacted. Perhaps more important is the availability of social media—your own blogs, Facebook, Twitter, etc.—to spread your words.

What is needed to secure change is the desire to do it. Getting the most from your legislature is not a passive activity. The signers of the Declaration of Independence were willing to risk their lives in defense of free legislatures. Are you willing to invest some effort to maintain them and make them fully functional in the public interest?

CONCLUSION

You do not have to be an Amanda Holt to have an impact on your state legislature and legislators. Few constituents have the luxury of the time to undertake a project of the magnitude of the legislative redistricting project that Ms. Holt undertook.

But you, the broader constituency, collectively have the ability to help things change for the better. You have a precious stake in the work of your legislature. As noted in the Introduction to this book, the education of your children, the condition of the highways you travel, the condition of the natural environment in which we exist, and many other matters of great importance are governed by what your legislature does.

It is easy to dismiss legislators and legislatures as just another group of politicians dawdling at the public expense. Scandals, apparently large salaries and benefits, seeming lobbyist control, and incumbent protective reapportionment of the state House and Senate and U.S. Congressional seats provide a seemingly good excuse to turn away. But that is only an excuse, not a valid justification.

However you view your state legislature, it is still one of the great institutions of constitutional government that evolved over eight centuries of English-American history. That is how the patriots who fought our American Revolution and wrote our U.S. Constitution saw it. That is why the U.S. Constitution calls for a "republican form" of government in the states, a form manifest through the creation of legislatures under each state constitution.

The legislative power comes from you, not those in the capitol. To bring your power as a constituent to bear on the legislature you cannot be satisfied to be a passive carper erupting in anger at the report of a legislative occurrence that outrages you. Such eruptions may be appropriate. But your ability to influence your House and Senate members will be strengthened by consistent communication with them on the basis of your own informed opinion.

Pay the same attention to legislators as you do to your tax returns. Form the habit of monitoring legislative activity by newspaper, radio, television, the Internet or social media. Make this a personal commitment as a citizen and do it with focus, curiosity and an open mind. Your perceptions may not be as valid as you think. Follow up with further research on issues through the websites and other information sources provided in this book. They are there for your use.

The public has never had more information available about the government and legislatures than it does now. Yet to this author, use of that information by the public appears to be barely tapped. That default cannot be blamed on the legislatures.

Bring your informed judgment to your legislators through thought-out expressions of your opinion in several ways:

- By direct contact. Send them a letter or make an appointment to visit them in their district office or at the capitol. If you vote in their district, they will not refuse to see you.
- Join with other constituents who share your interests and concerns. Organize your own citizens' committee on issues of concern, and act as a group.
- Establish a website and blog.
- Be sure you are registered to vote and vote in every election. Check with your qualified family members and friends. Encourage them to register and vote.
- Get involved in the election campaigns of those legislative candidates who share yours views. Give those candidates your help. The more help they have from their constituents, the less they need look elsewhere.

Being a successful candidate and effective legislator is not a solo endeavor, like golf or tennis. It requires a team effort, like football. Becoming part of the candidates "team" substantially increases your ability to influence the successful candidate.

If you do not choose to become involved in campaigns, your ability to influence is not lost. An effective constituency requires a participatory effort.

Figure 8.3. Rally at the Colorado capitol, 2013, celebrating marijuana legalization. Source: Rick Wilking/Reuters/CORBIS.

Everyone has to act, but the collective impact can bring new vitality and productivity to your legislature.

Thomas Jefferson and the other patriots who signed the Declaration of Independence pledged their lives and property for the cause of freely elected legislatures. If the signers of the Declaration made that strong a commitment to preserve freely elected legislatures, can you commit the time and interest necessary to help your state legislature achieve its full potential in our Constitutional framework?

You can do it and I hope you will.

NOTES

1. Occupy Harrisburg websites.
2. *The New York Times* (September 14, 2013), A17.
3. *Holt et al. v. 2011 Legislative Reapportionment Commission* P. S. Ct. (2012)
4. Ibid.
5. Ibid.
6. Amanda Holt, "The Public Needs to Engage in Latest Redistricting Map," *Harrisburg Patriot News* (April 22, 2012), C1.

IV

The Legislative Toolbox

Online and Organizational Information Sources

1. Every state legislature has a website that provides the basic information about it. All you have to do is Google "State Legislature of [state name]. For example, the Alabama State Legislature website provides links to Legislation, Code & Constitution; Senate live audio; House live audio; House members; Senate members; Profiled bills; Joint Interim Committees; Legislative process; House Rules; Senate Rules; Joint Rules; Legislative History; and Visitors' Guide.

Of course each state is different, but a good place to start for your state is the legislative website.

2. The best single source of information on legislatures from a national point of view is the National Conference of State Legislatures (NCSL), 7700 East First Place, Denver, CO 80230. Telephone 303/354–7700.

NCSL is the trade association of the 50 state legislatures and is staffed by several dozen professional and knowledgeable persons with considerable legislative experience. NCSL is continually studying state legislative issues and making available to the public the results of its studies. As indicated in the text of this book, NCSL has a website that is a national treasure trove of information on state legislatures. Go to www.NCSL.org.

One of the most valuable things NCSL does is post documents showing how the states compare on issues such as lobbying disclosure, campaign finances reporting, redistricting, etc. Although the NCSL exists to serve its members, the elected members of the 50 legislatures, its information is available to the public.

3. On money in state politics, the best source is the National Institute on Money in State Politics, 833 N. East Last Chance Gulch, Helena, Montana, 59601. Telephone 406/449–2480. This project operates a website,

www.followthemoney.org, that is a comprehensive overview and state-by-state report on how money is spent to influence legislatures. Its links include My District, Point of Influence, National Overview, Industry Influence, Timelines, and also a "Deeper focus" on subjects like independent spending. This project also has the only source of amounts spent on lobbying in some states.

4. The Pew Center on the States is devoted to the idea that "Good policy depends on good information." Its focus is on issues affecting state government generally, rather than on the legislatures themselves. It is located at 901 E Street, NW, Washington, DC 20004. Telephone: 202/552–2000. Its website is www.pewstates.org.

5. There are a number of websites on substantive legislative issues that provide a remarkable base of information on a state-by-state basis.

The Guttmacher Institute, for example, provides comprehensive and objective information on sexual and reproductive health and rights issues: www.Guttmacher.org. At this site, go to the "State Center" and you will find up-to-date information on all 50 states. Besides giving each state's provisions and pending proposals on the issues, the website has a variety of maps showing how states compare. The map below is a good example. Regardless

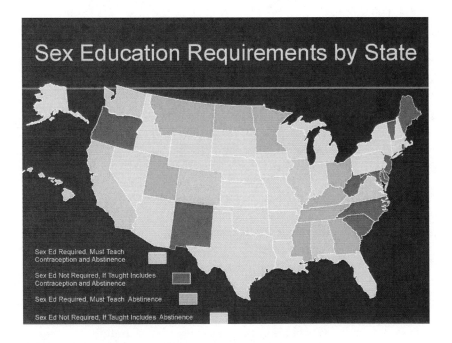

Guttmacher Institute map showing sexual education requirements in the states. Source: Guttmacher Institute website.

of your position on these issues, this site is an invaluable start on your research.

Another example is the Death Penalty Information Center (DPIC): www.deathpenaltyinfo.org. In addition to providing information on all aspects of death penalty issues, this site has a "State By State Database" that is vital to anyone researching issues related to the death penalty.

The Council on Governmental Ethics Laws (COGEL) is a professional organization for government agencies and other organizations working on ethics, elections, freedom of information, lobbying and campaign finance. See its website, www.cogel.org. COGEL sponsors conferences on these issues and provides monthly information on developments.

Bibliography and Suggestions
for Further Reading

CONSTITUTIONAL BACKGROUND

Bowen, Catherine Drinker. *Miracle at Philadelphia: The Story of the Constitutional Convention, May to September 1787*. Boston: Little, Brown and Company, 1966.
De Tocqueville, Alexis. *Democracy in America*. New York: Vintage Books, 1945.
Gutzman, Kevin R. *James Madison and the Marking of America*. New York: St. Martin's Press, 2012.
Hamilton, Alexander, James Madison, and John Jay. *The Federalist: A Commentary on the Constitution of the United States*. New York: Tudor Publishing Co., 1947.
Hindley, Geoffrey. The *Magna Carta. The Story of the Origins of Liberty*. Philadelphia: Running Press, 2008.
Howard, A. E. Dick. *Magna Carta: Text & Commentary*. Charlottesville: University of Virginia Press, 1998.
McCullough, David. *John Adams*. New York: Simon & Shuster, 2001.
Sydor, Charles S. *American Revolutionaries in the Making*. New York: Colliers Press, 1952.

CONTEMPORARY

Boyarsky, Bill. *Big Daddy: Jesse Unruh and the Art of Power Politics*. Los Angeles: University of California, 2008.
Broder, David S. *Democracy Derailed: Initiative Campaigns and the Power of Money*. New York: Harcourt Inc., 2000.
Bumsted, Brad. *Keystone Corruption: A Pennsylvania Insider's View of a State Gone Wromg*. Philadelphia: Camino Books, Inc., 2013.
Cannon, Lou. *Ronnie & Jesse: A Political Odyssey*. Garden City, NY: Doubleday & Co., 1969.
Kury, Franklin L. *Clean Politics, Clean Streams: A Legislative Autobiography*. Bethlehem, PA: Lehigh University Press, 2011.
Rosenthal, Alan. *Engines of Democracy: Politics and Policymaking in State Legislatures*. Washington, DC: CQ Press, 2006.
———. *The Decline of Representative Democracy. Process, Participation and Power in State Legislatures*. Washington, DC: CQ Press, 1998.

————. *The Third House. Lobbyists and Lobbying in the States*. Washington, DC: CQ Press, 2000.

Rosenthal, Alan, Karl T. Kurtz, John Hibbing, and Burden Loomis. *The Case for Representative Democracy: What Americans Should Know About their Legislatures*. Denver: National Conference of State Legislatures, 2001.

————. *Republic on Trial. The Case for Representative Democracy*. Washington, DC: CQ Press, 2003.

Schlesinger, Arthur M. Jr., *Crisis of the Old Order, 1919–1933*. Boston: Houghton Mifflin Company, 1957.

Squire, Perverell. *The Evolution of American Legislatures: Colonies, Territories and States, 1619–2009*. Ann Arbor: University of Michigan Press, 2012.

Readings for the Legislative Spirit

1. ARTICLE 61 OF THE MAGNA CARTA
(JUNE 1215)

61. SINCE WE HAVE GRANTED ALL THESE THINGS for God, for the better ordering of our kingdom, and to allay the discord that has arisen between us and our barons, and since we desire that they shall be enjoyed in their entirety, with lasting strength, for ever, we give and grant to the barons the following security:

The barons shall elect twenty-five of their number to keep, and cause to be observed with all their might, the peace and liberties granted and confirmed to them by this charter.

If we, our chief justice, our officials, or any of our servants offend in any respect against any man, or transgress any of the articles of the peace or of this security, and the offence is made known to four of the said twenty-five barons, they shall come to us—or in our absence from the kingdom to the chief justice—to declare it and claim immediate redress. If we, or in our absence abroad the chief justice, make no redress within forty days, reckoning from the day on which the offence was declared to us or to him, the four barons shall refer the matter to the rest of the twenty-five barons, who may distrain upon and assail us in every way possible, with the support of the whole community of the land, by seizing our castles, lands, possessions, or anything else saving only our own person and those of the queen and our children, until they have secured such redress as they have determined upon. Having secured the redress, they may then resume their normal obedience to us.

Any man who so desires may take an oath to obey the commands of the twenty-five barons for the achievement of these ends, and to join with them in assailing us to the utmost of his power. We give public and free permission to take this oath to any man who so desires, and at no time will we prohibit any man from taking it. Indeed, we will compel any of our subjects who are unwilling to take it to swear it at our command.

If anyone of the twenty-five barons dies or leaves the country, or is prevented in any other way from discharging his duties, the rest of them shall choose another baron in his place, at their discretion, who shall be duly sworn in as they were.

In the event of disagreement among the twenty-five barons on any matter referred to them for decision, the verdict of the majority present shall have the same validity as a unanimous verdict of the whole twenty-five, whether these were all present or some of those summoned were unwilling or unable to appear.

The twenty-five barons shall swear to obey all the above articles faithfully, and shall cause them to be obeyed by others to the best of their power.

We will not seek to procure from anyone, either by our own efforts or those of a third party, anything by which any part of these concessions or liberties might be revoked or diminished. Should such a thing be procured, it shall be null and void and we will at no time make use of it, either ourselves or through a third party.

2. EDMUND BURKE'S BRISTOL CONSTITUENCY SPEECH (EXCERPT); (NOVEMBER 3, 1774)

It ought to be the happiness and glory of a representative to live in the strictest union, the closest correspondence, and the most unreserved communication with his constituents. Their wishes ought to have great weight with;

their opinion high respect; their business unremitted attention. It is his duty to sacrifice his repose, his pleasures, his satisfaction, to theirs; and above all, even, and in all cases, to prefer their interest to his own.

Your representative owes you, not his industry only, but his judgment; and he betrays instead of serving you if he sacrifices it to your opinion.

3. THE DECLARATION OF INDEPENDENCE WITH REFERENCE TO COLONIAL LEGISLATURES AS JUSTIFICATION FOR INDEPENDENCE

IN CONGRESS, July 4, 1776

The unanimous Declaration of the thirteen united States of America,

When in the Course of human events, it becomes necessary for one people to dissolve the political bands which have connected them with another, and to assume among the powers of the earth, the separate and equal station to which the Laws of Nature and of Nature's God entitle them, a decent respect to the opinions of mankind requires that they should declare the causes which impel them to the separation.

We hold these truths to be self-evident, that all men are created equal, that they are endowed by their Creator with certain unalienable Rights, that among these are Life, Liberty and the pursuit of Happiness. That to secure these rights, Governments are instituted among Men, deriving their just powers from the consent of the governed, –That whenever any Form of Government becomes destructive of these ends, it is the Right of the People to alter or to abolish it, and to institute new Government, laying its foundation on such principles and organizing its powers in such form, as to them shall seem most likely to effect their Safety and Happiness. Prudence, indeed, will dictate that Governments long established should not be changed for light and transient causes; and accordingly all experience hath shewn, that mankind are more disposed to suffer, while evils are sufferable, than to right themselves by abolishing the forms to which they are accustomed. But when a long train of abuses and usurpations, pursuing invariably the same Object evinces a design to reduce them under absolute Despotism, it is their right, it is their duty, to throw off such Government, and to provide new Guards for their future security. –Such has been the patient sufferance of these Colonies; and such is now the necessity which constrains them to alter their former Systems of Government. The history of the present King of Great Britain is a history of repeated injuries and usurpations, all having in direct object the establishment of an absolute Tyranny over these States. To prove this, let Facts be submitted to a candid world.

He has refused his Assent to Laws, the most wholesome and necessary for the public good.

He has forbidden his Governors to pass Laws of immediate and pressing importance, unless suspended in their operation till his Assent should be obtained; and when so suspended, he has utterly neglected to attend to them.

He has refused to pass other Laws for the accommodation of large districts of people, unless those people would relinquish the right of Representation in the Legislature, a right inestimable to them and formidable to tyrants only.

He has called together legislative bodies at places unusual, uncomfortable, and distant from the depository of their public Records, for the sole purpose of fatiguing them into compliance with his measures.

He has dissolved Representative Houses repeatedly, for opposing with manly firmness his invasions on the rights of the people.

He has refused for a long time, after such dissolutions, to cause others to be elected; whereby the Legislative powers, incapable of Annihilation, have returned to the People at large for their exercise; the State remaining in the mean time exposed to all the dangers of invasion from without, and convulsions within....

For taking away our Charters, abolishing our most valuable Laws, and altering fundamentally the Forms of our Governments.

For suspending our own Legislatures, and declaring themselves invested with power to legislate for us in all cases whatsoever....

In every stage of these Oppressions We have Petitioned for Redress in the most humble terms: Our repeated Petitions have been answered only by repeated injury. A Prince whose character is thus marked by every act which may define a Tyrant, is unfit to be the ruler of a free people....

We, therefore, the Representatives of the united States of America, in General Congress, Assembled, appealing to the Supreme Judge of the world for the rectitude of our intentions, do, in the Name, and by Authority of the good People of these Colonies, solemnly publish and declare, That these United Colonies are, and of Right ought to be Free and Independent States; that they are Absolved from all Allegiance to the British Crown, and that all political connection between them and the State of Great Britain, is and ought to be totally dissolved; and that as Free and Independent States, they have full Power to levy War, conclude Peace, contract Alliances, establish Commerce, and to do all other Acts and Things which Independent States may of right do. And for the support of this Declaration, with a firm reliance on the protection of divine Providence, we mutually pledge to each other our Lives, our Fortunes and our sacred Honor.

Signed by John Hancock and 55 other patriots

4. ALEXIS DE TOCQUEVILLE ON AMERICAN STATE LEGISLATURES

LEGISLATIVE POWER OF THE STATE. *Division of the legislative body into two houses—Senate—House of Representatives—Different functions of these two bodies.*

The Legislative power of the state is vested in two assemblies, the first of which generally bears the name of the senate.

The Senate is commonly a legislative body, but it sometimes becomes an executive and judicial one. It takes part in the government in several ways, according to the constitution of the different states but it is in the nomination of public functionaries that it most commonly assumes an executive power. It partakes of judicial power in the trial of certain political offenses, and sometimes also in the decision of certain civil cases. The number of its members is always small.

The other branch of the legislature, which is usually called the House of Representatives, has no share whatever in the administration and takes a part in the judicial power only as it impeaches public functionaries before the Senate.

The members of the two houses are nearly everywhere subject to the same conditions of eligibility. They are chosen in the same manner, and by the same citizens. The only difference which exists between them is that the term for which the Senate is chosen is, in general, longer than that of the House of Representatives. The latter seldom remain in office longer than a year; the former usually sit two or three years.

By granting to the senators the privilege of being chosen for several years, and being renewed seriatim, the law takes care to preserve in the legislative body a nucleus of men already accustomed to public business, and capable of exercising a salutary influence upon the new-comers.

By this separation of the legislative body into two branches, the Americans plainly did not desire to make one house hereditary and the other elective, one aristocratic and the other democratic. It was not their object to create in the one a bulwark to power, while the other represented the interests and passions of the people. The only advantages that result from the present constitution of the two houses in the United States are the division of the legislative power, and the consequent check upon political movements; together with the creation of a tribunal of appeal for the revision of the laws.

Time and experience, however, have convinced the Americans that, even if these are its only advantages, the division of the legislative power is still a principle of the greatest necessity. Pennsylvania was the only one of the United States which at first attempted to establish a single House of Assembly, and Franklin himself was so far carried away by the logical consequences of the principle of the sovereignty of the people as to have concurred in the measure, but the Pennsylvanians were soon obliged to change the law and to create two houses. Thus the principle of the division of the legislative power was finally established, and its necessity may henceforward be regarded as a demonstrated truth. This theory, nearly unknown to the republics of antiquity, first introduced into the world almost by accident, like so many other great truths, and misunderstood by several modern nations, has at length become an axiom in the political science of the present age.

5. LEGISLATIVE CORRUPTION IN MONTANA (MONTANA SUPREME COURT EXCERPT)

Montana Supreme Court excerpt on Legislative Corruption (Western Tradition Partnership, Inc., et.al. vs. Attorney General of Montana, et. al., 2011 MT 328, p. 14–18):

22. Third, the Montana law at issue in this case cannot be understood outside the context of the time and place it was enacted, during the early twentieth century. (Montana became a state in 1889.) Those tumultuous years were marked by rough contests for political and economic domination primarily in the mining center of Butte, between mining and industrial enterprises controlled by foreign trusts or corporations.

These disputes had profound long-term impacts on the entire State, including issues regarding the judiciary, the location of the state capitol, the procedure for election of U.S. Senators, and the ownership and control of virtually all media outlets in the State.

23. Examples of well-financed corruption abound. In the fight over mineral rights between entrepreneur F. Augustus Heinze and the Anaconda Company, then controlled by Standard Oil, Heinze managed to control the two State judges in Butte, who routinely decided cases in his favor. K. Ross Toole, *Montana, An Uncommon Land* (Norman, OK: University of Oklahoma Press, 1959), 196–99. The Butte judges denied being bribed, but one of them admitted that Anaconda representatives had offered him $250,000 cash to sign an affidavit that Heinze had bribed him. Toole, *Montana,* 204.

24. In response to the legal conflicts with Heinze, in 1903 Anaconda/Standard closed down all its industrial and mining operations (but not the many newspapers it controlled), throwing 4/5 of the labor force of Montana out of work. Toole, *Montana,* 206. Its price for sending its employees back to work was that the Governor call a special session of the Legislature to enact a measure that would allow Anaconda to avoid having to litigate in front of the Butte judges. The Governor and Legislature capitulated and the statute survives. See e.g. *Patrick* v. *State,* 2011 MT 169, 17–23, 361 Mont. 204, 257 P.3d 365.

25. W. A. Clark, who had amassed a fortune from the industrial operations in Butte, set his sights on the United States Senate. In 1899, in the wake of a large number of suddenly affluent members, the Montana Legislature elected Clark to the U. S. Senate. Clark admitted to spending $272,000 in the effort and the estimated expense was over $400,000. Complaints of Clark's bribery of the Montana Legislature led to an investigation by the U. S. Senate in 1900. The Senate investigating committee concluded that Clark had won his seat through bribery and unseated him. The Senate committee "expressed horror at the amount of money which had been poured into politics in Montana elections . . . and expressed its concern with respect to the general aura of corruption in Montana." Toole, *Montana,* 186–94.

26. In a demonstration of extraordinary boldness, Clark returned to Montana, caused the Governor to leave the state on a ruse and, with assistance of the supportive Lt. Governor, won appointment to the very U. S. Senate seat that had just been denied him. Toole, *Montana,* 192–93. When the Senate threatened to investigate and unseat Clark a second time, he resigned. Clark eventually won his Senate seat after spending enough on political campaigns to seat a Montana Legislature favorable to his candidacy.

27. After the Anaconda Company cleared itself of opposition from Heinze and others, it controlled 90% of the press in the state and a majority of the legislature. C. B. Glasscock, *The War of the Copper Kings* (New York: Grosset & Dunlap, 1935), 290. By 1915 the company, after having acquired all of Clark's holdings as well as many others, "clearly dominated the Montana economy and political order ... [and] local folks now found themselves locked in the grip of a corporation controlled from Wall Street and insensitive to their concerns." Michael Malone and Richard Roeder, *Montana, a History of Two Centuries* (Seattle: University of Washington Press, 1976), 176. Even at that time it was evident that industrial corporations controlled the state "thus converting the state government into a political instrument for the furthering and accomplishment of legislation and the execution of laws favorable to the absentee stockholders of the large corporations and inimical to the economic interests of the wage earning and farming classes who constitute by far the larger percentage of the population in Montana." Helen Fisk Sanders, *History of Montana,* Vol. 1 (Chicago: Lewis Publishing Co., 1913), 429–30.

28. In 1900 Clark himself testified in the United States Senate that "[m]any people have become so indifferent to voting" in Montana as a result of the "large sums of money that have been expended in the state...." Toole, *Montana,* 184–85. This naked corporate manipulation of the very government (Governor and Legislature) of the State ultimately resulted in populist reforms that are still part of Montana law. In 1906 the people voted to amend the state Constitution to allow for voter initiatives. Not long thereafter, in 1906 this new initiative power was used to enact reforms including primacy elections to choose political candidates; the direct election of United States Senators; and the Corrupt Practices Act, part of which survives as § 13–35–227, MCA, at issue in this case.

29. The State of Montana was still contending with corporate domination even in the mid-20th century. For example, the Anaconda Company maintained controlling ownership of all but one of Montana's major newspapers until 1959. Writing in 1959, historian K. Ross Toole so noted and described the state:

Today the influence of the Anaconda Company in the state legislature is unspectacular but very great. It has been a long time since the company showed the mailed fist. But no informed person denies its influence or the fact that the basic use to which it is put is to maintain the status quo—to keep taxes down, not to rock the boat. Few of the company personnel either in Butte or in New York remember F. Augustus Heinze, or even for that matter, [U. S. Senator] Joseph M. Dixon, but it would be foolish for anyone to deny that the pervasive influence of the Anaconda Company in Montana politics is part and parcel of the Montana heritage. Toole, *Montana,* 244.

A study of Montana in the early 1970s concluded that corporate influence of the Anaconda Company had been "replaced by a corporate power structure, with interlocked directorates, the same law firms and common business interests" among the Anaconda Company, Montana Power Company, Burlington Northern Railway and the First Bank System. Malone and Roeder, *Montana, a History of Two Centuries,* 290. History professor Dr. Harry Fritz, in his affidavit presented in the District Court, affirmed that the "dangers of corporate influence remain in Montana" because the resources upon which its economy depends in turn depend upon distant markets. He affirmed: "What was true a century ago is as true today: distant corporate interests mean that corporate dominated campaigns will only work 'in the essential interest of outsiders with local interests a very secondary consideration.'" While specific corporate interests come and go in Montana, they are always present. Montana's mineral wealth, for example, has historically been exported from the State, and that is still true today. *Commonwealth Edison Co.* v. *State of Montana,* 189 Mont. 191, 196, 615 P.2d 847, 850 (1980), *aff'd,* 453 U.S. 609, 101 S. Ct. 2946. The corporate power that can be exerted with unlimited political spending is still a vital interest to the people of Montana.

6. AMANDA HOLT ON LEGISLATIVE REDISTRICTING, HARRISBURG PATRIOT NEWS, APRIL 22, 2012

It is the voice of each Pennsylvania resident that matters. It is the voice our constitution is designed to protect from dilution. Our constitution must not be compromised.

This means that counties, municipalities and wards must remain whole unless keeping another constitutional rule makes dividing unavoidable.

Redistricting, at least in Pennsylvania, was designed to ensure that people not only were offered equal representation but united representation. The latest proposals for redistricting should be reviewed by all voters with this standard in mind.

If people do not stay engaged with this redistricting process, then this protection of their voice might be lost as politicians strive to protect their incumbency.

The ability to select who represents us is at the core of why the United States was founded in the first place. People laid down their honor, fortunes and even lives to secure representation.

It mattered to them. It should matter to us.

Acknowledgments

Like a successful run for the state legislature, writing a book like this is not a solo endeavor like golf or tennis. Like football, it requires a team effort in which the ball carrier receives good support. I want to acknowledge with gratitude those who helped bring the book across the goal line of publication.

Dr. Shirley Anne Warsaw of Gettysburg College was instrumental in helping formulate the structure and focus and purpose. Vincent Carocci, who worked with me in the Senate and has published his own book, *A Capitol Journey*, gave the benefit of his experience through the process. On specific subjects I received the advice of Neil McAuliffe, former executive assistant to Senator Joseph Ammerman; Mark McKillop, legislative apportionment expert for the Senate minority; and Eric Fillman, attorney handling ethics matters for the House minority.

The National Conference of State Legislatures in Denver, Colorado, provided considerable source material, for which I want to pay a special thanks to its president, Bill Pound; Tim Storey, the program director; and former Colorado State Representative Peggy Kerns, an expert on state legislative ethical issues.

At Malady and Wooten where I work, I was provided review and encouragement by John Malady, Rick Wooten, and P.J. Lavelle, all of whom are exceptionally knowledgeable on legislatures and how they work. Micheline Leininger, the firm's office manager, was most helpful in resolving computer and copying problems.

Thanks too to Elizabeth Nash of the Guttmacher Institute for helpful suggestions and to Louis Riquelme of Corbis Images for his great work in providing many of the photographs used. Michele DeMary of Susquehanna University's Political Science Department provided encouragement. My sister Gloria Kury, who has significant publishing experience and now operates her own publishing company, Periscope Publishing, Ltd. (focused on art books), was especially helpful in working through the project and providing outstanding counsel from her experience.

Of course, through all of the project as well as my career, my wife Elizabeth has been indefatigably supportive and helpful. As a former editor of the University of Pittsburgh Law Review, her editorial skills have been fully employed in improving the manuscript.

To all of them I say, Thank you! Opinions expressed and any errors or mistakes are mine alone.

Franklin L. Kury

Index

About the Author

Franklin Kury brings to this book the unique perspective of one who has been both inside and outside of the legislature. As a teenager he watched his father twice run for the Pennsylvania House of Representatives and lose both times. In college he was a member of the Trinity College delegation to the Connecticut Intercollegiate Student Legislature for four years. While a law student he worked as a reporter for his hometown paper (*The Sunbury Daily Item*) where he interviewed and reported on the area state House members. Elected to the Pennsylvania House of Representative for three terms and two terms to the State Senate, he retired voluntarily in 1980. In the House he was the author of the environmental rights amendment to the Pennsylvania constitution. In the Senate he chaired the committee that reformed the process for Senate confirmation of gubernatorial nominations and the committee that reformed the Public Utility Commission, including the creation of a consumer advocate. As a lawyer with Reed Smith, and now as a lobbyist with Malady & Wooten, a Harrisburg government affairs firm, he advises clients on the state legislature and advocates on their behalf. In 2011, *Clean Politics, Clean Streams: A Legislative Autobiography* was published by the Lehigh University Press. In December 2013 the Pennsylvania Supreme Court cited that book twice and used excerpts from it for the plurality opinion in the *Robinson Township* case. This opinion is a landmark environmental law decision that infuses new vitality into Art. 1, Sec. 27—the environmental rights amendment—to the state constitution. He is married to the former Elizabeth Heazlett of Pittsburgh and they are the parents of three sons. His personal website is www.franklinkury.com.

About the Author

Franklin Kury. Source: Author's file.